LIBRARY AND
INFORMATION SOURCES
ON WOMEN

CONTRIBUTING EDITORS

Rose Anne Burstein, Sarah Lawrence College (Chairperson)

Lynn S. Mullins, Rutgers, The State University of New Jersey, Newark (Coordinating Editor)

●

Susanne Garrett, State University of New York, College at Purchase

Janice Gordon-Kelter, Center for the Study of Women and Society, The Graduate School and University Center of The City University of New York

Carol Greenholz, State University of New York, College of Technology at Farmingdale

Lynne Karen, College of New Rochelle

Ida Lowe, Baruch College of The City University of New York

Patricia Profeta, Rutgers, The State University of New Jersey, Newark

Gurley Turner, Gossage Regan Associates, Inc.

Sue Rosenberg Zalk, Center for the Study of Women and Society, The Graduate School and University Center of The City University of New York

LIBRARY AND INFORMATION SOURCES ON WOMEN

A Guide to Collections
in the Greater New York Area

Compiled and Edited by
The Women's Resources Group of the Greater New York
Metropolitan Area Chapter of the Association of
College and Research Libraries
and
the Center for the Study of Women and Society of
the Graduate School and University Center of
the City University of New York

The Feminist Press at The City University of New York
New York

To the members of the ACRL/NY Executive Board, past and present, for their encouragement and support

Published 1988 by The Feminist Press at The City University of New York, 311 East 94 Street, New York, N.Y. 10128

Distributed by The Talman Company, Inc., 150 Fifth Avenue, New York, N.Y. 10011

91 90 89 88 5 4 3 2 1

Library of Congress Cataloging-in-Publication Data
Library and information sources on women: a guide to collections in the Greater New York area / compiled and edited by the Women's Resources Group of the Greater New York Metropolitan Area Chapter of the Association of College and Research Libraries and the Center for the Study of Women and Society of the Graduate School and University Center of the City University of New York.
    p. cm.
  Includes index.
  ISBN 0-935312-88-9 (pbk.) : $12.95
    1. Women—Information services—New York (N.Y.)—Directories. 2. Women—Research—New York (N.Y.)—Information services—Directories. 3. Information services—New York (N.Y.) I. Association of College and Research Libraries. Greater New York Metropolitan Area Chapter. Women's Resources Group. II. City University of New York. Center for the Study of Women and Society.
HQ1181.U5L52 1987
305.4′025′7471—dc19   87-35068
                                                                              CIP

This book was made possible in part by funds granted by the Charles H. Revson Foundation. The statements made and views expressed, however, are solely the responsibility of the author.

Text design by Paula Martinac
Printed in the United States of America

CONTENTS

PREFACE

Recent years have witnessed an extraordinary increase in the scholarship addressing the history, status, concerns, and roles of women. The need for a comprehensive directory of information sources on women has been evident for some time to scholars, researchers, reference librarians, and many others seeking this information. Since seventy-eight percent of the research libraries in New York State are located in the greater New York metropolitan area, the need for a guide to women's resources in this region is particularly strong. *Library and Information Sources on Women: A Guide to Collections in the Greater New York Area* has been compiled to address this need.

This book is a guide to 171 collections on women in the five boroughs of New York City; Long Island; Westchester County; and eastern New Jersey. The collections are housed in a varied group of organizations—special libraries, libraries of historical societies and government agencies, public and academic libraries, and other organizations that hold resources on women. This is the first time that many of these institutions have been listed in a directory of resources for research on women.

The directory is arranged alphabetically by the name of the institution containing the collection, with cross-references provided for ease of use. Collection entries are numbered sequentially. Each entry contains the following information, as applicable: name and address, telephone number, contact person, objectives of library or information center, access privileges, hours, description of women's materials, collection by format, services, publications, and additional information.

Although contact names, hours, and access privileges have been verified as close as possible to publication date, the nature of these collections make them vulnerable to change. Users are advised to call before attempting to access some of the smaller collections. The book includes a detailed subject index, with subject headings based on a *Women's Thesaurus* (developed by the National Council for Research on Women), supplemented by terms generated by a Key Word in Context (KWIC) index. Browsing through the guide and its subject index may prove to be a good way for the reader to become acquainted with the depth and scope of the directory.

Many people contributed to the development and production of this directory. A prototype, entitled *A Guide to Collections on Women in the New York Area*, was compiled in 1980 by Martha Nelson and Jan Clausen of the Center for the Study of Women and Sex Roles at the Graduate School of the City

University of New York. It was a slim, photocopied publication, but it proved to be popular to area researchers since it was the only available source for locating specific resource collections on women in the New York metropolitan area. The Greater New York Metropolitan Area Chapter of the Association of College and Research Libraries (ACRL) became involved in 1983 when Chapter President Sarah Watstein, currently at Hunter College, focused attention on the need for an expanded edition of the guide.

The Center for the Study of Women and Society at the Graduate School and University Center of The City University of New York was contacted and interest was expressed in the undertaking of the project. Rose Anne Burstein, Library Director at Sarah Lawrence College, assumed the leadership of the project. In 1985, under her direction, the chapter and the center formed a Women's Resources Group to compile and edit the directory. The members of the Women's Resources Group are as follows: Rose Anne Burstein, Sarah Lawrence College (Chairperson); Susanne Garrett, SUNY at Purchase; Carol Greenholz, SUNY at Farmingdale; Lynne Karen, College of New Rochelle; Ida Lowe, Bernard M. Baruch College; Lynn S. Mullins, Rutgers University, Newark; Patricia Profeta, Rutgers University, Newark; Gurley Turner, Gossage Regan Associates; and Sue Rosenberg Zalk and Janice Gordon-Kelter, Center for the Study of Women and Society, Graduate School and University Center, CUNY.

As Chairperson of the Women's Resources Group, Rose Anne Burstein provided a vision and strong sense of direction that made possible the successful completion of the project. She spearheaded the planning for the directory and was instrumental in the raising of funds and, with Sue Rosenberg Zalk, in the selection of a publisher.

In 1986, the Charles H. Revson Foundation, believing that there was a need for the directory and in their wish to support research and study on the concerns of women, awarded the group $5,000 to aid in the publication. At the same time, The Feminist Press at The City University of New York agreed to publish the guide. Throughout the entire project, the Greater New York Area ACRL Executive Board was extremely supportive, allocating funds and encouraging the group to continue its efforts.

A questionnaire was developed and listings of libraries believed to have resources of value were compiled. The sources used to identify these organizations were: the mailing lists of the New York City Commission on the Status of Women and the Westchester Commission on the Status of Women; the directories of the New York Metropolitan Reference and Research Library Agency (METRO), Special Libraries Association (SLA), and the Westchester Library Association. Long Island and New Jersey libraries and historical societies that were probable owners of women's collections were also added to the list. The selection was based on the judgment of the various members of the group, with the assistance of Carol Greenholz, Susanne Garrett, and Patricia Profeta, for the identification of libraries in Long Island, Westchester County, and New Jersey. The questionnaires were mailed and the returns were monitored by Sue Zalk and Janice Gordon-Kelter. Lynn S. Mullins did the editing of the responses, a process that involved the review of the questionnaires and accompanying supporting materials and the writing of a large number of the entries. Lynn Mullins also served as coordinator of the project in 1987. The data entry was done by Brady Earnhart and James Charlton, then of Marymount Manhattan College. The entry descriptions were returned to the respondents for review and correction under the supervision of Susan Gleason and Edith Liszewski of Sarah Lawrence College. A second mailing was sent out to libraries that had not responded, and telephone calls were made by Gurley Turner, Lynne Karen, and Carol Greenholz to additional libraries, urging them to participate in the project. The indexing was done by Ida Lowe, Susanne Garrett, and Carol Greenholz, with the assistance of James Charlton. The technical aspects of word processing and indexing were overseen by Ida Lowe.

The Women's Resources Group is grateful to the many librarians who took the time to make their holdings on women's studies more widely known. It recognizes that there may be other libraries with important holdings that are not included in the guide, and suggests that these libraries contact The Feminist Press for possible inclusion in a new edition should one be forthcoming.

LIBRARY AND
INFORMATION SOURCES
ON WOMEN

A. A. BRILL LIBRARY

see New York Psychoanalytic Institute

●

ABRAHAM STONE MEMORIAL LIBRARY

see Planned Parenthood of New York City

●

ADAM AND SOPHIE GIMBEL DESIGN LIBRARY

see Parsons School of Design

1. ADELPHI UNIVERSITY

Swirbul Library
Reference Department
Garden City, New York 11530

Telephone Number

(516) 663-1036

Contact Person

Carol F. Schroeder, Reference Coordinator.

Objectives of Library or Information Center

To support the curriculum of Adelphi University.

Access Privileges

Open to the public.

Hours

Monday through Thursday, 8:00–11:00; Friday, 8:00–9:00; Saturday, 9:00–9:00; Sunday, 1:00–11:00.

Description of Women's Materials

The collection is a general one, with emphasis on the social aspects of women's studies.

Collection by Format

Books and monographs: 1,000
Government documents: 500
Pamphlets: 7 vols.
Reprints, clippings: 3 vols.
Audiotapes: 30

Videotapes: 10
Films: 9
Slides: yes
Kits: 1
Current serial titles: 8

Services

Borrowing privileges: yes
Interlibrary loan: yes
Telephone reference: yes

Reading room: yes
Photocopying: yes
Audiovisual facilities: yes

2. THE ALAN GUTTMACHER INSTITUTE

111 Fifth Avenue
New York, New York 10003

Telephone Number

(212) 254-5656, ext. 202

Contact Person

Susan Tew, Public Information Specialist.

Objectives of Library or Information Center

To promote public policies and programs that will enable the avoidance of unintended pregnancy and the achievement of childbearing goals.

Access Privileges

Open to the public by telephone and mail. The Alan Guttmacher Institute does not have a formal library or resource/information center. It does, however, provide data by telephone and by mail.

Description of Women's Materials

The Institute has data/information in the following subject areas: abortion services in the United States and worldwide; teenage pregnancy; maternal health; contraceptive services/practice/research and development/funding; government funding/policies in reproductive health care; and sex education.

Collection by Format

Books and monographs: yes

Services

Telephone reference: yes

Publications

Finding aids/guides: The Institute publishes three periodicals, *Family Planning Perspectives, International Family Planning Perspectives,* and *Washington Memo.* It also publishes a number of titles on family planning services and methods, abortion politics, teenage pregnancy, etc., and *Issues in Brief.*

Additional Information

The Alan Guttmacher Institute was founded in 1968 as a semi-autonomous division of the Planned Parenthood Federation of America. It became an independent nonprofit corporation for research, policy analysis, and public education in 1977. In this capacity, it serves a broad constituency of opinion leaders, public officials, and lawmakers, as well as the general public concerned with the complex policy and practical issues related to human reproduction. The Institute has a two-fold mission: to promote, through the gathering and dissemination of information, enlightened public policies for the provision of family planning services and reproductive health care; and to see that these policies are translated into effective and cost-efficient programs sensitively designed to meet the needs of consumers. It has accomplished these goals through a unique combination of research, policy analysis, and publishing activities that identify and shed light on poorly understood issues as they arise.

•

ALLIANCE FRANCAISE LIBRARY

see French Institute

3. AMALGAMATED CLOTHING AND TEXTILE WORKERS UNION

Research Department Library
15 Union Square
New York, New York 10003-3377

Telephone Number

(212) 242-0700

Contact Person

Henrietta Dabney, Director of Research.

Objectives of Library or Information Center

To serve as a resource for the research staff of the ACTWU.

Access Privileges

Open to the public by appointment.

Description of Women's Materials

The Library of the ACTWU Research Department has relatively few resources of value on women's studies. The archives of its predecessor union, the Amalgamated Clothing Workers of America, which includes the Bessie Hillman Papers, are in the Labor Management Documentation Center at Cornell University. The locations of the archives of other predecessor unions (the Textile Workers Union of America, the United Textile Workers of America, and the United Hatters, Cap, and Millinery Workers International Union) are located at various institutions which are specified in the *Selected Bibliography of the Amalgamated Clothing and Textile Workers Union* (1986). There are, however, a large number of general and historical volumes on the Union that are still located in New York. They deal with such issues as imports, organizing (the J. P. Stevens organizing drive), occupational safety and health, plant closings, productivity and technological change, and sociological and psychological studies. Information on women is not singled out, but is included as part of the collection.

Publications

Bibliographies: *Selected Bibliography of the Amalgamated Clothing and Textile Workers Union* (1986).

4. AMERICAN ACADEMY AND INSTITUTE OF ARTS AND LETTERS LIBRARY

633 West 155 Street
New York, New York 10032

Telephone Number

(212) 368-6361

Contact Person

Nancy Johnson, Librarian.

Objectives of Library or Information Center

To collect books, musical recordings and scores, manuscript material and letters pertaining to the artists, writers, and composers who are or have been members of the organization since its founding in 1898.

Access Privileges

Open to college-level researchers by appointment. Fees for photocopying only.

Hours

Monday through Friday, 9:30–5:00 by appointment; July and August, 10:00–4:00 by appointment.

Description of Women's Materials

Major subjects of interest are literature, fine arts, music, and cultural history. The collection is not limited to women's studies, but includes books, records, musical scores, exhibition catalogs, files of correspondence, memorabilia, and manuscripts relating to twentieth-century women artists, writers, and composers who have been members of the organization. Deceased women members of the Institute or the Academy (or both) include Hannah Arendt, Djuna Barnes, Elizabeth Bishop, Louise Bogan, Catherine Drinker Bowen, Pearl S. Buck, Rachel Carson, Willa Cather, Babette Deutsch, Edna Ferber, Janet Flanner, Edith Hamilton, Lillian Hellman, Malvina Hoffman, Julia Ward Howe, Helen Keller, Carson McCullers, Margaret Mead, Edna St. Vincent Millay, Marianne Craig Moore, Alice Neel, Anaïs Nin, Georgia O'Keefe, Dorothy Parker, Muriel Rukeyser, Edith Wharton, and Marguerite Yourcenar, among others. Current women members include artists Isabel Bishop, Helen Frankenthaler, Louise Nevelson, writers Kay Boyle, Hortense Calisher, Joan Didion, Elizabeth Hardwick, Ada Louise Huxtable, Mary McCarthy, Toni Morrison, Grace Paley, Susan Sontag, Eudora Welty, and composers Vivian Fine, Miriam Gideon, and Betsy Jolas, among others. Also on file are records of the debate over the admission of women as members.

Collection by Format

Books and monographs: 20,000
Archives: yes
Files of correspondence: yes
Manuscripts: yes

Press clippings: yes
Photographs relating to members: yes

Please call or write for detailed descriptions of holdings relating to a particular woman member.

Services

Interlibrary loan: yes
Telephone reference: yes

Reading room: yes
Photocopying: yes

Publications

Finding aids/guides: Card index to library and archives.

5. AMERICAN FRIENDS SERVICE COMMITTEE

Information Services
15 Rutherford Place
New York, New York 10003

Telephone Number

(212) 598-0972

Contact Person

Laurel Hayes.

Description of Women's Materials

The American Friends Service Committee has a bookstore, rather than a library. There are very few resources on women. However, there are two programs that are directed at specific groups of New York women: the Cambodian Women's Project (Heang Char, 598-0968), and the Haitian Women's Project (598-0965). The former Project seeks to provide survival skills workshops for Cambodian women. It serves an advocacy and bridge role with health and social service providers to interpret traditional Cambodian approaches to mental and physical health. There is a newsletter issued in Cambodian and English, and a videotape. The latter Project seeks to provide similar workshops in such areas as nutrition, health services, housing, immigration problems, and employment. There is a series of pamphlets. Additionally, the Committee's Community Relations division held a conference on the feminization of poverty several years ago, and a transcript is available for $5.00.

Collection by Format

Books and monographs: yes
Pamphlets: yes
Videotapes: yes

Films: yes
Filmstrips: yes
Slides: yes

6. AMERICAN JEWISH COMMITTEE

Blaustein Library
165 East 56 Street
New York, New York 10022

Telephone Number

(212) 751-4000, ext. 297

Contact Person

Cyma Horowitz, Library Director.

Objectives of Library or Information Center

The Library is concerned with American Jewish life—human rights, intergroup relations, interreligious relations, and contemporary Jewish communities in the United States and in other parts of the world.

Access Privileges

Open to qualified individuals by appointment.

Hours

Monday through Friday, 9:30–5:30.

Description of Women's Materials

The collection deals with Jewish women in the family, in religious life, and in communal life, reflecting both historic and contemporary views.

Collection by Format

Books and monographs: 75
Current serial titles: 6

7. AMERICAN JOURNAL OF NURSING CO.

Sophia F. Palmer Library
555 West 57 Street
New York, New York 10019

Telephone Number

(212) 582-8820

Contact Person

Frederick Pattison, Beth Mills.

Access Privileges

Open to graduate students only; call for an appointment.

Hours

Monday through Friday, 10:00–4:00.

Description of Women's Materials

The Library contains resources on nurses or nursing and related allied health areas.

Collection by Format

Books and monographs: yes
Current serial titles: yes

Services

Borrowing privileges: reference only
Telephone reference: limited
Reading room: yes
Photocopying: yes

Interlibrary loan: photocopies of journal articles, Regional Medical Library coupons only

Publications

Finding aids/guides: Publishes the *International Nursing Index* in cooperation with the National Library of Medicine. The *International Nursing Index* also includes *Nursing Citation Index.*

8. AMERICAN MUSEUM OF NATURAL HISTORY

Central Park West at 79 Street
New York, New York 10024

Telephone Number

(212) 769-5400

Contact Person

Department of Library Services.

Objectives of Library or Information Center

To support the work of the Museum's scientific staff and to serve the scientific and scholarly community. Offers limited access to its collection of serials, monographs, photographs, films, and Museum archives.

Access Privileges

Open to the public (closed stacks). METRO referral card honored. Appointment necessary for use of Special Collections.

Hours

Monday through Friday, 11:00–4:00; Wednesday, till 8:30.

Description of Women's Materials

The Library contains biographical information on women scientists and explorers. There are also anthropological and sociological treatises on the treatment and social conditions of women, birth customs, and motherhood, as well as broader works on social structures, the family, marriage and divorce, dress and adornment, and sex roles, relations, and customs.

Collection by Format

Books and monographs: yes   Slides: yes
Films: yes   Manuscripts or archives: yes

The Mary Jobe Akeley field journals and papers collection is of note.

Services

Photocopying: yes   Reading room: yes
Interlibrary loan: yes   Audiovisual facilities: yes

9. AMERICAN NUMISMATIC SOCIETY LIBRARY

Broadway at 155 Street
New York, New York 10032

Telephone Number

(212) 234-3130, ext. 20

Contact Person

Francis D. Campbell, Librarian.

Objectives of Library or Information Center

The collection and cataloging of monographs, journals, and journal articles pertaining to numismatics for the purpose of furthering research.

Access Privileges

Open to the public.

Hours

Tuesday through Saturday, 9:00–4:30.

Description of Women's Materials

Monographs, pamphlets, and articles treating women as depicted on coins, medals, paper money, etc. Approximately fifty items in these categories have been cataloged. Collection includes titles such as *Women's Advancement and Money* (n.d.), *Canadian Women and Medals* (1980), and *Efigii Feminine pe Monedele Romane* (1983).

Collection by Format

Books and monographs: yes
Reprints, clippings: yes
Pamphlets: yes

Services

Interlibrary loan: restricted
Reading room: yes
Photocopying: restricted

Mail reference: yes
Audiovisual facilities: microfilm

ARCHIBALD STEVENS ALEXANDER LIBRARY

see Rutgers, The State University of New Jersey

10. ASSOCIATION FOR VOLUNTARY SURGICAL CONTRACEPTION

Library
122 East 42 Street
New York, New York 10168

Telephone Number

(212) 351-2504

Contact Person

William J. Record.

Objectives of Library or Information Center

To promote voluntary surgical sterilization.

Access Privileges

Open to the public by appointment. METRO referral card honored.

Hours

Monday through Friday, 9:00–5:00.

Description of Women's Materials

Sexual sterilization and related problems, e.g., family planning.

Collection by Format

Books and monographs: 3,000
Current serial titles: 100
Government documents: ca. 120
Pamphlets: ca. 120

Reprints, clippings: 80 feet
Videotapes: 40
Films: 80

Services

Interlibrary loan: yes
Telephone reference: yes
Reading room: yes

Publications

Accession lists: yes

Additional Information

The Association for Voluntary Surgical Contraception has publications available at no charge, e.g., *Biomedical Bulletin* and *AVSC News*. Organizations may ask to be placed on the mailing list.

11. THE ASSOCIATION OF JUNIOR LEAGUES— RESOURCE CENTER

825 Third Avenue
New York, New York 10022

Telephone Number

(212) 355-4380

Contact Person

Tom Littler.

Objectives of Library or Information Center

To maintain archives of the Association and to provide a core collection of materials on volunteering, women, and children.

Access Privileges

Open to qualified researchers or writers.

Hours

By appointment.

Description of Women's Materials

The archives of the Association detail the activities of a prominent women's organization since the inception of the Association in 1901. Although the book collection on women is not large, it contains many essential feminist writings.

Collection by Format

Books and monographs: 150
Government documents: 50
Current serial titles: 20

Pamphlets: 300
Manuscripts or archives: large holdings

The archives are of particular interest to social historians.

Services

Photocopying: yes
Reading room: yes

12. AUSTRALIAN CONSULATE-GENERAL

Australian Reference Library
636 Fifth Avenue, Fourth Floor
New York, New York 10111

Telephone Number

(212) 245-4000, ext. 217 or 215

Contact Person

Jill Hutchison, Michele Weinreich.

Objectives of Library or Information Center

To provide a resource of current and historical information on Australia.

Access Privileges

Open to the public.

Hours

Monday through Friday, 10:00–1:00 and 2:00–4:00, except holidays.

Description of Women's Materials

The Library contains books, pamphlets, newsletters, clipping files of newspaper and magazine articles, statistics, directories, ministerial press releases, parliamentary reports, etc., on Australia. The subjects covered include history, social issues, health, literature, the arts, education, migrant women, women in politics and government, women in the work force (statistics, special industries, equal pay, affirmative action legislation).

Collection by Format

Books and monographs: yes
Current serial titles: yes
Pamphlets: yes
Reprints, clippings: yes (from major
   Australian papers and magazines)

Government documents: yes (ministerial press releases and parliamentary reports)

Services

Borrowing privileges: some books—one-week loan (with driver's license identification)
Interlibrary loan: yes
Reading room: yes

THE BACKLASH TIMES

see Feminists Fighting Pornography

13. BARNARD COLLEGE LIBRARY

3009 Broadway
New York, New York 10027-6598

Telephone Number

(212) 280-3953

Contact Person

Natalie Sonevytsky, Reference Librarian.

Objectives of Library or Information Center

To support the curriculum of a liberal arts college for women with a strong program in women's studies.

Access Privileges

Open to persons with valid Columbia University identification (including Research Libraries Group members). METRO referral card honored.

Hours

Monday through Thursday, 8:45 A.M.–10:00 P.M.; Friday, 8:45–6:00; Saturday, 12:00–5:00; Sunday, 1:00–6:00 during academic semester. At other times, generally Monday through Friday, 9:00–5:00. Call for an appointment for evenings and weekends.

Description of Women's Materials

Materials on women are dispersed throughout the general collection in both the humanities and the social sciences. Except in foreign literatures, most are in English. Special collections include the Overbury Collection (American women authors from Anne Bradstreet to the present), the Gabriela Mistral Collection (the personal library of the Chilean poet), and the College Archives.

Collection by Format

Books and monographs: ca. 3,000
Manuscripts or archives: ca. 400 feet
Overbury and Mistral Collections total about 4,000 vols.

Services

Borrowing privileges: with ID
Interlibrary loan: yes
Telephone reference: yes

Reading room: yes
Photocopying: yes
Audiovisual facilities: yes

Publications

Bibliographies: *Women's Studies: Basic Reference Sources and Other Resources at Barnard.*
Finding aids/guides: *Catalog of the Gabriela Mistral Collection.*

14. THE BARNARD WOMEN'S CENTER

Birdie Goldsmith Ast Resource Collection
3009 Broadway
New York, New York 10027

Telephone Number

(212) 280-2067

Contact Person

Lucinda Manning.

Objectives of Library or Information Center

The Barnard Women's Center is a community of scholars and a clearinghouse for scholarly information in the area of women's studies. The Birdie Goldsmith Ast Resource Collection includes special collections, books, conference papers, articles, feminist periodicals, bibliographies, handbooks, and directories that cover the scope of international women's studies.

Access Privileges

Open to the public and the academic community.

Hours

Monday through Friday, 9:00–5:00.

Description of Women's Materials

The collection includes materials on arts and culture, education, employment, health and fitness, legal status, women in other countries, sex roles and sex differences, violence and sexual exploitation, women and development, the women's movement, and feminist theory. Each major division is divided into five to seven subdivisions. Of special interest is the Ruth Milkman Collection on Comparable Worth.

Collection by Format

Books and monographs: yes
Current serial titles: yes
Government documents: yes
Pamphlets: yes

Reprints, clippings: yes
Audiotapes: yes
Oral history: yes
Manuscripts or archives: yes

Audiotapes are based on programs sponsored by The Barnard Women's Center. These include tapes of lectures/papers presented at Women's Issue Luncheons, Conversations about Women, Women's History Seminars, and the annual Scholar and the Feminist Conference. The Birdie Goldsmith Ast Resource Collection is an international center for clippings, unpublished conference papers, and books dealing with every aspect of women's lives. The Center subscribes to eighty periodicals and newsletters from Europe, Asia, Africa, and Latin America, as well as the United States. In addition to the general materials, there is a growing collection on women in the arts, Third World women, immigrants and refugees, the international peace movements, and reproductive rights and the new reproductive technologies. There are some eight thousand items in the collection.

Services

Photocopying: yes
Reading room: yes

Publications

Publications that have come out of activities at The Barnard Women's Resource Center include the *Directory of Research on Women* (for all of Columbia University) coordinated by The Barnard Women's Center and The University Committee on Women's Studies (co-conveners Temma Kaplan and Marsha Wright), The Barnard Women's Center (1985), *Pleasure and Danger: Exploring Female Sexuality,* edited by Amy Swerdlow and Hanna Lessingried (1984), and *The Future of Difference,* edited by Hester Eisenstein and Alice Jardine (1980, 1985). These and other publications are available in the collection for researchers to use on premises. *The Directory of Research* and *The Barnard Occasional Papers* are available for purchase.

15. BETTYE LANE

Studio 501 D
155 Bank Street
New York, New York 10014

Telephone Number

(212) 243-4213

Contact Person

Bettye Lane.

Objectives of Library or Information Center

Documentation in photographs and written material of the women's movement from 1969 to the present.

Access Privileges

Open to researchers, editors, writers, etc. Fees depend upon the use of photographs and other material.

Hours

Call for an appointment.

Description of Women's Materials

Bettye Lane is a widely published photojournalist who has photographed the demonstrations, conferences, events, and leaders of the women's movement.

Collection by Format

Books and monographs: yes
Pamphlets: yes
Government documents: yes

Reprints, clippings: yes
Slides: yes
Manuscripts or archives: yes

The slide show, "A Room of One's Own," documents the women's movement.

Publications

Finding aids/guides: There are listings of subjects covered by Bettye Lane's photographs under such broad categories as women's rights activities, conferences, demonstrations, lesbians, marches, professional and blue collar workers, women in sports, and personalities, each category of which is further subdivided by specific events, issues, or individuals.

THE BILLY ROSE THEATRE COLLECTION

see The New York Public Library at Lincoln Center

●

BIRDIE GOLDSMITH AST RESOURCE COLLECTION

see The Barnard Women's Center

●

BLAUSTEIN LIBRARY

see American Jewish Committee

16. BRAMSON ORT TECHNICAL INSTITUTE

44 East 23 Street
New York, New York 10010

Telephone Number

(212) 677-7420

Contact Person

Marjorie Scal, Librarian.

Objectives of Library or Information Center

To collect materials on computers, electrical engineering, ophthalmic technology, and Judaica.

Access Privileges

Open to Bramson students. METRO referral card honored.

Hours

Monday through Thursday, 9:00–5:00; Friday, 9:00–12:00.

Description of Women's Materials

The Institute includes materials on sex roles and on the role of the Jewish woman and the Jewish wife.

Collection by Format

Books and monographs: yes
Current serial titles: yes

Services

Telephone reference: yes
Interlibrary loan: yes

17. BRONX COMMUNITY COLLEGE LIBRARY

Bronx, New York 10453

Telephone Number

(212) 220-6076; 220-6077

Contact Person

Julie Skurdenis.

Objectives of Library or Information Center

To serve the community college students and faculty.

Access Privileges

Open to City University students and faculty.

Hours

Monday through Thursday, 9:00–9:00; Friday, 9:00–5:00; Saturday, 10:00–3:00.

Description of Women's Materials

The College's women's collection is of a general nature.

Collection by Format

Books and monographs: yes
Current serial titles: yes
Government documents: yes
Pamphlets: yes
Reprints, clippings: yes
Microfilm reels: yes

Audiotapes: yes
Videotapes: yes
Films: yes
Filmstrips: yes
Slides: yes

Services

Borrowing privileges: yes
Photocopying: yes
Interlibrary loan: yes

Reading room: yes
Audiovisual facilities: yes

18. BROOKHAVEN NATIONAL LABORATORY

Women in Science Collection
Research Library 477A
Upton, New York 11973

Telephone Number

(516) 282-3487; 282-5202

Contact Person

Rosemary Cohen.

Objectives of Library or Information Center

To accumulate information for women in the sciences concerning jobs, salaries, management, and women's studies.

Access Privileges

Open to members of the Women in Science Group at Brookhaven National Laboratory and other employees.

Hours

Monday through Friday, 8:30–5:00.

Description of Women's Materials

The Research Library has a small collection of books, journals, newsletters, and government publications on women scientists/professionals. The collection is, for the most part, career-goal and management oriented.

Collection by Format

Books and monographs: 50
Current serial titles: 10
Government documents: 50

Pamphlets: 20
Reprints, clippings: 20

Services

Borrowing privileges: yes

Publications

Accession lists: *WIS Newsletter.*

Additional Resources

The Technical Information Division has a special collection on management that is non-sex oriented and that is for the use of all employees interested in management. This collection includes material on women as managers.

Additional Information

The collection is very small and belongs to the Women in Science Club, but is housed in the Research Library. Women in Science members may borrow for extended periods of time, and new publications are listed in the *Newsletter*. Tapes of talks given by women scientists and other professionals are a part of the collection.

19. BROOKLYN COLLEGE LIBRARY

Bedford Avenue and Avenue H
Brooklyn, New York 11210

Telephone Number

(718) 780-5342

Contact Person

Renee Feinberg.

Objectives of Library or Information Center

To support the College curriculum.

Access Privileges

Open to members of CUNY, SUNY, and Academic Libraries of Brooklyn only; valid identification card required. METRO referral card honored.

Hours

Monday through Thursday, 9:00 A.M.–9:45 P.M.; Friday, 9:00–4:45; Saturday and Sunday, 12:00–4:45 during academic semester.

Description of Women's Materials

The Library has a basic collection of women's resources.

20. BROOKLYN LAW SCHOOL LIBRARY

250 Joralemon Street
Brooklyn, New York 11201

Telephone Number

(718) 780-7974

Contact Person

Linda Holmes.

Objectives of Library or Information Center

To support the educational and research needs of the Brooklyn Law School students, faculty, and alumni.

Access Privileges

Open to Brooklyn Law School students, faculty, and (paid) alumni; public has access to government documents collection. METRO referral cards honored. Fees: $300.00 per year for other attorneys.

Hours

Monday through Friday, 8:00 A.M.–12:00 midnight; Saturday, 9:00–9:00; Sunday, 9:00 A.M.–11:00 P.M. Shorter hours during summer and holidays.

Description of Women's Materials

The Library has resources on women's legal status; discrimination in all aspects of society (courts, employment, laws, etc.); the role of women throughout legal history; and international legal issues regarding women.

Collection by Format

Books and monographs: yes
Current serial titles: yes
Government documents: yes

Services

Telephone reference: yes
Interlibrary loan: yes

21. THE BROOKLYN MUSEUM

Art Reference Library
200 Eastern Parkway
Brooklyn, New York 11238

Telephone Number

(718) 638-5000, ext. 308

Contact Person

Deirdre E. Lawrence.

Objectives of Library or Information Center

To provide a research center for documentation on the Brooklyn Museum Collections and on related areas.

Access Privileges

Open to the public. METRO referral card honored.

Hours

Wednesday through Friday, 1:00–4:30.

Description of Women's Materials

Contains research material on women artists and their art. Includes files from the *Feminist Art Journal.*

Collection by Format

Books and monographs: 100   Pamphlets: 200
Current serial titles: 2   Reprints, clippings: 100

Services

Telephone reference: yes   Reading room: yes
Photocopying: yes   Audiovisual facilities: yes
Interlibrary loan: yes

THE BURKE LIBRARY

see Union Theological Seminary

●

22. BUTTERICK COMPANY, INC.

The Fashion Information Center
161 Sixth Avenue
New York, New York 10013

Telephone Number

(212) 620-2518

Contact Person

Cindy Rose.

Objectives of Library or Information Center

To collect materials on fashion, color, and fabric forecasting.

Access Privileges

Open to retail accounts and manufacturers.

Hours

Monday through Friday, 9:00–5:00.

Collection by Format

Pamphlets: yes
Audiotapes: yes
Videotapes: yes

Filmstrips: yes
Slides: yes
Manuscripts or archives: yes

Services

Reading room: yes
Audiovisual facilities: yes

23. CALDWELL COLLEGE LIBRARY

Ryerson Avenue
Caldwell, New Jersey 07006

Telephone Number

(201) 228-4424, ext. 312

Contact Person

Reference Librarian.

Objectives of Library or Information Center

To provide curriculum-related informational resources to students, faculty, staff, and researchers.

Access Privileges

Open to the public for on-site use.

Hours

Call.

Description of Women's Materials

The collection encompasses the women's movement, women authors, artists, the history and condition of women in the United States and in foreign nations, women in religion, ethnic perspectives, and business and economics.

Collection by Format

Books and monographs: ca. 1,700
Other: A few multimedia kits

Services

Interlibrary loan: yes
Reading room: yes

24. CATALYST INFORMATION CENTER

250 Park Avenue South
New York, New York 10003

Telephone Number

(212) 777-8900, ext. 352

Contact Person

Susan Barribeau.

Objectives of Library or Information Center

To collect and review materials pertaining to the careers and leadership development of women.

Access Privileges

Open to the public by appointment. METRO referral card honored.

Hours

Monday through Friday, 9:00–5:00.

Description of Women's Materials

The materials on women and management and on leadership roles are of primary importance. Parenting issues, two-career families and the corporate response, pay equity, sexual harassment, laws and legislation affecting women in the workplace, sex roles, women's achievements, and women in professional fields are a key part of the collection.

Collection by Format

Books and monographs: 3,500
Current serial titles: yes
Government documents: yes

Pamphlets: yes
Reprints, clippings: yes
Other: extensive vertical files

There is also a collection of statistical information that is of note.

Services

Photocopying: yes

Publications

Accession lists: yes

25. CENTER FOR ARTS INFORMATION

1285 Avenue of the Americas, Third Floor
New York, New York 10019

Telephone Number

(212) 977-2544

Contact Person

Tom Damrauer, Director of Library.

Objectives of Library or Information Center

The Center for Arts Information was established in 1976 as a comprehensive information service for the nonprofit arts community. The Center's primary objective is the collection and dissemination of information concerning services, programs, and funds to aid in the management, production, and presentation of the nonprofit arts.

Access Privileges

Open to the public by appointment.

Hours

Monday, Tuesday, Thursday, 11:00–5:00; Wednesday, 11:00–7:00.

Description of Women's Materials

The research library houses a collection of arts management information for professional artists and managers of nonprofit arts organizations. There are books cataloged under the subject heading "Women in the Arts" and a clipping file of materials on the same subject. This subject encompasses information on funding sources for women artists and women's art organizations, and information on women managers in the museum profession.

Collection by Format

Books and monographs: yes
Current serial titles: yes
Reprints, clippings: yes

The library is predominantly an arts management collection that includes bibliographies, directories, research studies, and standard texts. It also includes annual reports and other documents from the National Endowment for the Arts, the New York State Council on the Arts, other government agencies, and some foundations and corporations. There are some five hundred files on service organizations and funding agencies, containing information on the programs and services of each. The subject files contain clippings, magazine articles, press releases, and ephemeral materials on over two hundred and fifty subjects. There are some three hundred arts management periodicals and newsletters.

Services

Telephone reference: yes
Photocopying: yes
Reading room: yes

Publications

The Center publishes a variety of arts directories—*Artist Colonies* (1986); *Jobs in the Arts and Arts Administration* (1984); *Money for Artists* (1987); *International Cultural Exchange* (1985); management aids; a quarterly newsletter, *For Your Information,* which contains practical information for those who create and work in the arts; and a real estate monthly, *Spaces.* It also sponsors *A Guide for Video and Filmmakers* (1987).

●

CENTER FOR LABOR STUDIES

see Empire State College

26. CENTER FOR MEDICAL CONSUMERS

237 Thompson Street
New York, New York 10012

Telephone Number

(212) 674-7105

Contact Person

Maryann Napoli, Associate Director.

Objectives of Library or Information Center

To help people make informed medical treatment decisions.

Access Privileges

Open to the public.

Hours

Monday, Tuesday, Thursday, Friday, 9:00–5:00; Wednesday, 9:00–7:00.

Description of Women's Materials

The Center is not focused exclusively on women's health, but several shelves of books and a large portion of the files are on this topic.

Collection by Format

Books and monographs: 50   Pamphlets: hundreds
Government documents: some   Reprints, clippings: large files

Services

Photocopying: yes
Reading room: yes

Additional Information

Established in 1976, the library of the Center for Medical Consumers was the first free medical library for laypeople. Over fifteen hundred books and periodicals are available for reference. These include medical and scientific texts and journals, as well as publications written for the general public. There is a substantial amount of material on alternative approaches to health and illness. The Center's information desk maintains files to help callers find other sources of information and help whenever possible. The Center publishes *HealthFacts*, a monthly consumer newsletter that is intended to determine the need, risks, and effectiveness of various medical practices and nonmedical alternatives.

27. CENTER FOR MIGRATION STUDIES LIBRARY/ARCHIVES

209 Flagg Place
Staten Island, New York 10304

Telephone Number

(718) 351-8800

Contact Person

Diana J. Zimmerman, Director.

Objectives of Library or Information Center

To be a specialized library dealing primarily with migration and refugees worldwide and, secondarily, with ethnicity and ethnic group relations. The archival collections relate mainly to the Italian immigration and ethnic experience.

Access Privileges

Open to the public.

Hours

Monday through Friday, 9:00–5:00.

Description of Women's Materials

The collection of women's materials focuses on migration-related topics, ethnicity, and the role of women in other countries and cultures.

Collection by Format

Books and monographs: 200
Government documents: 10
Microfilm reels: 8 (dissertations)

In addition to the above, women are frequently dealt with in edited volumes on migration, in materials concerning specific ethnic groups, in the refugee literature, and the like.

Services

Telephone reference: limited
Photocopying: yes
Reading room: yes

Audiovisual facilities: microfilm
reader-printer

Additional Information

The Center for Migration Studies devoted a special issue in each of its journals to the topic of women in migration: *International Migration Review* 18 (Winter 1984) and *Migration Today* 10, nos. 3/4 (1982). *Migration Today* was changed to *Migration World* as of 1986 (14, nos. 1/2). The first issue was a special issue on women. In addition, *Migration Today* frequently contains articles dealing with women immigrants and refugees.

●

CENTER FOR WOMEN IN GOVERNMENT

see State University of New York at Albany

●

CENTER OF ALCOHOL STUDIES

see Rutgers, The State University of New Jersey

28. CHURCH WOMEN UNITED

475 Riverside Drive
New York, New York 10115

Telephone Number

(212) 870-2347

Contact Person

Doris Anne Younger, General Director.

Objectives of Library or Information Center

Church Women United is a national movement of Protestant, Roman Catholic, Orthodox, and other Christian women.

Access Privileges

Open to researchers by appointment.

Description of Women's Materials

The materials include back volumes of the organization's periodical, sets of minutes, and additional archival holdings of an organization that has been a powerful force for justice issues since its founding in 1941.

Collection by Format

Books and monographs: yes
Current serial titles: yes
Manuscripts or archives: yes

Arrangements have been made for the use of the resources of the Presbyterian Church, in Philadelphia, for the storage of the archives of Church Women United. Work has to be done, however, on the organization of the archives before any transfer can be made.

29. THE CITY COLLEGE OF THE CITY UNIVERSITY OF NEW YORK

Library
Convent Avenue and 138 Street
New York, New York 10031

Telephone Number

(212) 690-4292

Contact Person

Sheila R. Herstein, Collection Development Coordinator.

Objectives of Library or Information Center

To support the curriculum of a large urban academic institution.

Access Privileges

Open to City University of New York students, faculty, and staff, and the community, for research purposes. METRO referral card honored.

Hours

Monday through Thursday, 9:00 A.M.–10:00 P.M.; Friday, 9:00–5:00; Saturday, 12:00–6:00; Sunday, 2:00–6:00.

Description of Women's Materials

Good collection of college-level women's materials, including in-depth coverage of women's history, education, feminist theory, women's socialization and sex roles, literature, etc. The collection is rich in secondary source materials for racial and ethnic groups as well. Included within the Russell Sage Collection, a unique archival source in social welfare, are important materials on child welfare, women and social agencies, women and volunteerism, and marriage and the family—primarily materials of a historical nature.

Collection by Format

It is difficult to estimate the size of the collection, since this is an integrated collection and the material falls in a variety of Library of Congress classes. However, it should be noted that the collection has been growing since the college opened in 1847 and is comprehensive.

Services

Borrowing privileges: for CUNY only
Interlibrary loan: yes
Telephone reference: yes

Photocopying: on-site
Audiovisual facilities: yes
Reading room: no separate facility

30. THE CITY UNIVERSITY OF NEW YORK

Central Office Library and Archives
535 East 80 Street
New York, New York 10021

Telephone Number

(212) 794-5510

Contact Person

Paul Perkus.

Objectives of Library or Information Center

To provide information to administrators and trustees of the University.

Access Privileges

Open to bona fide researchers, by appointment only. METRO referral card honored.

Hours

Monday through Friday, 9:00–5:00; closed on Fridays during the summer.

Description of Women's Materials

There are no specific collections of women's materials. The Archives contain records of the Board of Higher Education, the Board of Trustees, and the Central Administration of the City University of New York from ca. 1930–1980. These collections might be of interest from the standpoint of women's studies.

31. THE CITY UNIVERSITY OF NEW YORK

The Graduate School and University Center
Mina Rees Library
33 West 42 Street
New York, New York 10036

Telephone Number

(212) 790-4541

Contact Person

Susan Newman, Chief Readers' Services Librarian.

Objectives of Library or Information Center

Primarily to support the course work of the doctoral programs in humanities, social sciences, and mathematics.

Access Privileges

On-site privileges to those who have need to use the collection. METRO referral card honored.

Hours

Academic semester: Monday through Thursday, 9:00–9:00; Friday, 9:00–5:00. Summer: Monday through Friday, 9:00–5:00.

Collection by Format

Books and monographs: 1,000
Current serial titles: 10

Collection includes recent publications of The Feminist Press and relevant City University of New York doctoral dissertations.

Services

Telephone reference: limited   Interlibrary loan: yes
Photocopying: yes   Reading room: yes

Publications

List of periodicals received includes those on women's resources.

32. THE COLLEGE OF INSURANCE LIBRARY

101 Murray Street
New York, New York 10007

Telephone Number

(212) 962-4111

Contact Person

Beverly Rosignolo.

Objectives of Library or Information Center

To provide information on insurance, insurance-related subjects, and the insurance industry.

Access Privileges

Open to the general public for reference use only. METRO referral card honored.

Hours

Monday through Thursday, 10:00–9:00; Friday, 10:00–5:00.

Description of Women's Materials

The collection includes material on women in insurance and on old-age pensions and social insurance for women.

Collection by Format

Books and monographs: yes
Current serial titles: yes

Government documents: yes
Other: vertical files

Services

Reading room: yes

33. COLLEGE OF NEW ROCHELLE

Gill Library
New Rochelle, New York 10801

Telephone Number

(914) 632-5300, ext. 347

Contact Person

James T. Schleifer.

Objectives of Library or Information Center

To support the College's curriculum, and to provide timely information to the general public.

Access Privileges

On-site use for all but high school students. METRO referral card honored.

Hours

Monday through Thursday, 8:30 A.M.–11:00 P.M.; Friday, 8:30–5:00; Saturday, 9:00–5:00; Sunday, 11:00–11:00.

Description of Women's Materials

The resources on women are cataloged as part of the general collection. The majority of volumes are under the classification Women. Feminism, HQ 1101–HQ 2030.7. Additional materials appear in the catalog under the headings Women and Religion, Women in Literature, Women—Employment, Women—Sexual Behavior, Women in Art, Women Scientists, and Women's Health.

Collection by Format

Books and monographs: 860
Current serial titles: 23
Pamphlets: 200
Audiotapes: 21
Videotapes: 1
Filmstrips: 2
Manuscripts or archives: 200

The archives contain significant materials concerning higher education for women in New York State.

Services

Telephone reference: yes
Photocopying: yes
Interlibrary loan: yes
Reading room: yes

Publications

Accession lists: yes
Periodicals received: yes
Bibliographies: yes

●

COLUMBIA UNIVERSITY

see also Women's National Book Association

34. COLUMBIA UNIVERSITY LIBRARIES

535 West 114 Street
New York, New York 10027

Telephone Number

(212) 280-2241

Contact Person

Reference Department, Butler Library.

Objectives of Library or Information Center

Open to students, faculty, and other active members of the University. Researchers and scholars not affiliated with the University may utilize the collection under certain guidelines. Applications should be addressed to the Library Information Office (234 Butler Library). METRO referral card honored.

Hours

Hours vary from department to department.

Description of Women's Materials

Columbia does not have a specific separate women's studies collection; all materials are classified by Library of Congress in the departmental libraries.

Collection by Format

The Rare Book and Manuscript Library (Sixth Floor, Butler Library) contains extensive primary materials on the various aspects of women's studies. Correspondence, documents, manuscripts, reports, and related materials exist in the collections of prominent individuals such as Frances Perkins, Elizabeth Blackwell, Lillian Wald, and Mary E. Richmond; in organizational collections such as the League of Women Voters and the Women's National Book Association; and in other collections not primarily concerning women. There are description sheets (and in some cases detailed inventories) for each collection of papers; important correspondence and manuscripts from women are also cataloged separately in all collections.

Services

Borrowing privileges: yes
Audiovisual facilities: yes
Telephone reference: yes (limited)

Photocopying: yes
Interlibrary loan: yes
Reading room: yes

Publications

Bibliographies: *Selected Bibliography on Women's Studies* (1984).

Additional Resources

Columbia's Oral History Office collection contains interviews with Frances Perkins and Millicent Fenwick, among many others.

●

COMMISSION ON THE STATUS OF WOMEN

see New York City Commission on the Status of Women

35. COOPER-HEWITT MUSEUM LIBRARY AND ARCHIVES

2 East 91 Street
New York, New York 10128

Telephone Number

(212) 860-6883/6887

Contact Person

Katharine Martinez, Chief Librarian.

Objectives of Library or Information Center

To serve the research, exhibition, and education programs of the Cooper-Hewitt Museum, the Smithsonian Institution's National Museum of Design.

Access Privileges

Open to adult researchers. METRO referral card honored.

Hours

Monday through Friday, 10:00–5:30.

Description of Women's Materials

Includes resources on women artists in the fields of decorative arts, textiles, architecture, and design; women in the home (interior decoration); objects designed for women; and women's costume accessories.

Collection by Format

Books and monographs: yes
Pamphlets: yes
Current serial titles: yes
Microfilm reels: yes
Microfiche: yes

Slides: yes
Manuscripts or archives: yes
Other: Therese Bonney archive of
   photographs.

Services

Telephone reference: yes
Photocopying: yes
Interlibrary loan: yes

Reading room: yes
Audiovisual facilities: microfiche and
   film readers

36. COOPER UNION LIBRARY

41 Cooper Square
New York, New York 10003

Telephone Number

(212) 254-6300, ext. 329

Contact Person

Ulla Volk.

Objectives of Library or Information Center

The pertinent material is contained within the Cooper Collection, a library/ archive established to preserve the personal papers of Peter Cooper and Abram S. Hewitt, along with related documents and other sources concerned with the history of Cooper Union and New York City.

Access Privileges

Open to scholars, graduate students, writers, and other researchers. METRO referral card honored.

Hours

Monday through Friday, 9:00–5:00; summers, Monday through Thursday.

Description of Women's Materials

A believer in education for women, Peter Cooper established the Women's Art School as one of the original divisions of his Union. Therefore, the early annual reports of the school, along with his opinions on education for women contained in copies of his speeches, etc., are sometimes consulted by researchers. Additionally, as the Great Hall of Cooper Union served as a platform for women's rights agitation during the post-Civil War period, some researchers seek information on the speechmaking at Cooper Union.

Collection by Format

Books and monographs: yes | Reprints, clippings: yes
Pamphlets: yes | Manuscripts or archives: yes

Services

Telephone reference: limited to brief questions
Photocopying: yes
Reading room: yes

Additional Information

There are a few items that may be of particular interest. The collection contains a letter from Susan Anthony to Sarah Cooper Hewitt (March 16, 1888), asking her to lead the singing at a meeting of the International Council of Women (Washington, D.C., March 25–April 1, 1888). There is also a letter from Anthony to Cooper (May 1870) requesting return of the $40.00 deposit made by the Woman Suffrage Society for the use of the Great Hall. A summary of the speechmaking by nineteenth-century feminists at Cooper Union is contained in Richard Ek's *A Historical Study of the Speechmaking at Cooper Union, 1859–1897* (Ph.D. dissertation, 1964, University of Southern California), pp. 406–24. A copy of the work is contained within the Cooper Collection.

37. CORNELL UNIVERSITY/NEW YORK STATE SCHOOL OF INDUSTRIAL AND LABOR RELATIONS

Sanford V. Lenz Library
15 East 26 Street
New York, New York 10010

Telephone Number

(212) 340-2845

Contact Person

Nancy J. Furlan, Librarian.

Objectives of Library or Information Center

To serve as a resource center for courses offered at Cornell's Metropolitan District.

Access Privileges

Open to the public.

Hours

During the school year, hours vary depending upon courses offered. Summer hours: Monday through Thursday, 9:00–5:00. Please call.

Description of Women's Materials

The Library is essentially labor oriented. The women's collection is a part of the labor materials. Within the women's materials are biographies, materials on women and labor, labor history (with an emphasis on women in labor history), comparable worth, and ethnic studies. There is also a vertical file of women's materials. Also included is a small collection of oral histories.

Collection by Format

Books and monographs: yes
Current serial titles: yes
Government documents: yes
Reprints, clippings: many
Audiotapes: yes

Oral history: yes
Films: available through Ithaca campus
Manuscripts or archives: possibly available through Ithaca campus

Services

Borrowing privileges: students only
Telephone reference: yes
Photocopying: yes

Interlibrary loan: yes
Reading room: yes

Publications

Finding aids/guides: Subject headings list for women's vertical file.

38. CORNELL UNIVERSITY/NEW YORK STATE SCHOOL OF INDUSTRIAL AND LABOR RELATIONS

Working Women's Institute
15 East 26 Street, Fourth Floor
New York, New York 10010

Telephone Number

(212) 340-2840

Contact Person

K.C. Wagner.

Objectives of Library or Information Center

To collect information relating to sexual harassment, sex discrimination, conditions of work, and Titles VII and IX.

Description of Women's Materials

The collection contains materials on women and work and the issues of sexual harassment and sex discrimination.

Collection by Format

Books and monographs: yes   Pamphlets: yes
Current serial titles: yes   Reprints, clippings: yes
Government documents: yes

Additional Information

In January 1986, the Working Women's Institute became a part of Cornell University. Founded in 1975, the Working Women's Institute is a national research, training, and consultation center. Its focus is on equal employment opportunities for women—most specifically, the impact of sexual harassment and gender bias on working women. Building on a decade of research, policy analysis, counseling, and education, the Institute has created a program to help any organization prevent sexual harassment and gender bias. Over the years it has worked with corporations, universities, human service organizations, unions, women's groups, and attorneys.

39. THE COUNCIL OF THE CITY OF NEW YORK

Committee on Women
Miriam Friedlander, Chairwoman
Council Member 2nd District, Manhattan
City Hall
New York, New York 10007

Telephone Number

(212) 566-1324

Contact Person

Pamela Elam, Legislative Aide.

Objectives of Library or Information Center

The New York City Council Committee on Women has held hearings on issues related to women since the creation of the Committee in 1983.

Access Privileges

Call for an appointment.

Hours

Monday through Friday, 9:30–5:00.

Description of Women's Materials

Hearings have been held on such subjects as day care for city workers, comparable worth, sex discrimination in insurance, the problems of homeless women, the impact of office automation on working women, businesswomen and city contracts, improving the status of women and minorities in the New York City government, the feminization of poverty, women and sports, and services to victims of domestic violence. Copies of reports and resolutions are available.

40. CREATIVE WOMEN'S COLLECTIVE

618 Sixth Avenue
New York, New York 10011

Telephone Number

(212) 924-2184

Contact Person

Jackie Skiles.

Access Privileges

Open to the public by appointment. Fees: $5.00 donation.

Hours

Monday through Friday, mainly afternoons and evenings.

Description of Women's Materials

There are materials on the arts, on women's rights in general, and on events and issues in the New York area. The emphasis is on ephemeral materials on the women's movement—flyers, newsletters, announcements of events, films, posters. The collection, however, is neither cataloged nor organized, other than a rough arrangement by year.

Collection by Format

Reprints, clippings: some
Manuscripts or archives: yes
Other: flyers, letters, photos, posters (500–1,000 pieces); some newsletters

The material relating to the Creative Women's Collective itself documents the efforts of this women artists' group to create and distribute (and help others do the same with their materials) graphics relating to women's issues and social change.

Services

Photocopying: yes

Additional Information

The Creative Women's Collective is a nonprofit organization of women artists—painters, sculptors, graphic artists, photographers, and others—who show a commitment to issues of concern to women and to positive social change. Its members have been collaborating on educational and art projects since 1973. They collectively design and screenprint graphics on women's issues and social change and assist others to design and silkscreen their own T-shirts, posters, etc. The Collective is especially interested in helping organizations that need to commission graphics for fundraising and communication purposes. The studio may be rented at a reasonable fee by artists and organizations for producing their own work. Currently serving as artists-in-residence at The Door youth center (where free classes are offered to its members), the Collective also offers silkscreen classes for adults. The group designs its own "Special Edition" line of feminist and social change T-shirts.

41. DREW UNIVERSITY LIBRARY

Madison, New Jersey 07940

Telephone Number

(201) 377-3000, ext. 588 (Reference Service)

Contact Person

Ruth Friedman.

Objectives of Library or Information Center

To serve the College of Liberal Arts, Graduate, and Theological Schools.

Access Privileges

Open to non-Drew community for use of materials in the Library only. Fees: Borrower's card—$25.00 per year.

Hours

During regular fall semester: Monday through Thursday, 8:00–12:00 (midnight) with reference service 9:00–5:00 and 7:00–10:00; Friday, 9:00–5:00. Summer and January hours vary.

Description of Women's Materials

The collection includes basic reference sources and indexes to support an undergraduate minor in women's studies. Broad coverage. No particular in-depth areas. Circulating collection also broad. United States government depository collection available for loan. Some nineteenth-century materials.

Collection by Format

Books and monographs: yes
Current serial titles: yes
Government documents: yes

Pamphlets: yes
Reprints, clippings: yes

Services

Telephone reference: yes
Audiovisual facilities: yes

Photocopying: yes
Interlibrary loan: yes

Publications

Bibliographies: *Reference Sources on Women.*

EAGLETON INSTITUTE OF POLITICS, CENTER FOR THE AMERICAN WOMAN AND POLITICS

see Rutgers, The State University of New Jersey

●

42. EDUCATIONAL EQUITY CONCEPTS, INC.
114 East 32 Street, Suite 306
New York, New York 10016

Telephone Number

(212) 725-1803

Contact Person

Merle Froschl.

Objectives of Library or Information Center

To provide information on issues of women and disability. Intend to develop a national clearinghouse on information, programs, and projects.

Access Privileges

Call for information.

Description of Women's Materials

Materials on women and disability.

Collection by Format

Books and monographs: yes
Pamphlets: yes
Reprints, clippings: yes

Services

Telephone reference: yes

●

ELIAS LIEBERMAN HIGHER EDUCATION CONTRACT LIBRARY

see National Center for the Study of Collective Bargaining in Higher Education and the Professions

43. ELIZABETH SETON COLLEGE LIBRARY

1061 North Broadway
Yonkers, New York 10701

Telephone Number

(914) 969-4000, ext. 287

Contact Person

Sister Margaret Sullivan.

Objectives of Library or Information Center

Curriculum-oriented to assist students doing research and reference.

Access Privileges

METRO referral card honored.

Hours

Monday through Thursday, 8:30 A.M.–10:00 P.M.; Friday, 8:30–5:00. Weekend college session: Saturday, 10:00–5:00; Sunday, 11:00–5:00. Non-weekend college session: Saturday, 1:00–5:00; Sunday, 1:00–5:00.

Description of Women's Materials

The collection of women's materials is small but it generally covers a diversity of areas.

Collection by Format

Books and monographs: 95
Current serial titles: 14
Pamphlets: 25

Audiotapes: 2
Films: 2
Filmstrips: 3 sets

Services

Photocopying: yes
Interlibrary loan: yes
Audiovisual facilities: yes

44. EMPIRE STATE COLLEGE

Center for Labor Studies
330 West 42 Street
New York, New York 10036

Telephone Number

(212) 279-7380, ext. 20

Contact Person

Jayne Adler.

Objectives of Library or Information Center

To provide a specialized labor studies collection concerned with workers and work, particularly with unionized workers.

Access Privileges

Open to the public for reference use.

Hours

Monday through Thursday, 2:00–8:00; hours subject to change.

Description of Women's Materials

There are limited holdings on women and labor history, on trade union activity regarding pay equity, child care, maternity leave, and on apprenticeships in nontraditional jobs.

Collection by Format

Books and monographs: 30
Government documents: ca. 25
Audiotapes: 1
Slides: 1 set

Other: Bureau of National Affairs *Labor Relations Reference* volumes have important and timely applications.

There are some eighty trade-union newspapers that have material of general and specific interest that might be useful for research on women and labor. There is also a collection of nonunion produced periodicals of labor interest.

Services

Photocopying: yes

45. ENDOMETRIOSIS ASSOCIATION

The Greater New York Chapter
420 East 66 Street, Box 22
New York, New York 10021

Telephone Number

(212) 861-4327

Contact Person

Yolanda Santiago, President.

Objectives of Library or Information Center

To assist women with endometriosis and others in exchanging information about endometriosis, to educate the public and medical community about the disease, and to promote research related to endometriosis.

Description of Women's Materials

The Greater New York Chapter was the first local chapter to be chartered by the Endometriosis Association, in 1982. The Chapter is in the initial stages of developing a library.

Publications

The Association publishes a newsletter and a number of other publications.

●

ESTHER RAUSHENBUSH LIBRARY

see Sarah Lawrence College

46. FASHION INSTITUTE OF TECHNOLOGY

Library
227 West 27 Street
New York, New York 10001

Telephone Number

(212) 760-7590

Contact Person

Marjorie Miller, Reference.

Objectives of Library or Information Center

To provide resource material to the FIT community and to outside researchers.

Access Privileges

Open to the public by appointment. METRO referral card honored.

Hours

Monday through Thursday, 9:00 A.M.–10:00 P.M.; Friday, 9:00–8:00; weekend hours during semester only.

Description of Women's Materials

The basic interest for women's studies is in the costume and fashion fields—retrospective and current biographical material about women in all aspects of the fashion and related industries. Special Collections holds rare material in costume.

Collection by Format

Books and monographs: 10,000
Current serial titles: 100
Reprints, clippings: 100 vertical files

Videotapes: 50
Oral history: 15 tapes

The vertical file collection is unique. It contains extensive materials on fashion industry people that are not found in other sources.

Services

Telephone reference: yes
Photocopying: yes

Interlibrary loan: yes
Reading room: yes

47. THE FEMINIST PRESS AT THE CITY UNIVERSITY OF NEW YORK

311 East 94 Street
New York, New York 10128

Telephone Number

(212) 360-5790

Contact Person

Florence Howe.

Objectives of Library or Information Center

This is a "potential" collection, in need of a trained librarian and catalogs.

Access Privileges

Not usable at the moment except in rare cases.

Description of Women's Materials

There is a collection of books on women, with many resources from other countries. There are also ephemera from all regions and most countries in the world. Feminist journals, many complete from the 1960s, topical vertical files, and women's studies files for all colleges and universities in the United States, from the late 1960s to the present, are included.

Collection by Format

Books and monographs: yes
Current serial titles: yes
Government documents: yes

48. FEMINISTS FIGHTING PORNOGRAPHY
The Backlash Times
P.O. Box 6731
Yorkville Station
New York, New York 10128

Telephone Number

(212) 410-5182

Contact Person

Page Mellish.

Objectives of Library or Information Center

The Backlash Times is a magazine containing some fifty newsbriefs on pornography culled from the press and other media.

Access Privileges

Subscriptions are $15.00; $3.00 per issue.

Description of Women's Materials

The Backlash Times is a news service on pornography and violence against women, women fighting back, and sexism in media. The activists of Feminists Fighting Pornography monitor the press and some one thousand magazines and clip pertinent items for publication in *The Backlash Times.*

Collection by Format

Reprints, clippings: ca. 50 newsclips per issue of *The Backlash Times*
Slides: yes

There is a slideshow on pornography available for showing by Feminists Fighting Pornography for $75.00 (for sale at $100.00). It is shown to women once a month at The Women's Center, 243 West 20 Street, New York, between Seventh and Eighth Avenues ($5.00 contribution includes tour of 42 Street).

Additional Information

The Backlash Times is of particular interest to researchers, activists, lawyers, legislators, and teachers. It chronicles legislation, legal cases, statistics, surveys, and the like, on the issues of pornography, images of women, violence against women, sexual abuse, advertising, sexism in mass media, women fighting back, prostitution, and female sexual slavery.

49. THE FERTILITY AWARENESS CENTER/BIRTH CONTROL OR ACHIEVING PREGNANCY—THE NATURAL WAY

342 East 15 Street
New York, New York 10003

Telephone Number

(212) 475-4490

Contact Person

Barbara Feldman, Director.

Objectives of Library or Information Center

To provide a resource for reproductive health information with focus on nat-ural/holistic alternatives not usually offered by the medico-pharmaceutical mainstream. The Center's motto: "Everyone has the right to know all the alternatives."

Access Privileges

Open to individuals. Fees per individual situation.

Hours

By appointment.

Description of Women's Materials

Resources on natural methods of birth control, available and experimental artificial birth control, abortion, infertility, and pre-pregnancy health, preg-nancy, female and male reproductive health problems, and the role of nutri-tion in reproductive health.

Collection by Format

Books and monographs: yes
Pamphlets: yes

Reprints, clippings: yes
Audiotapes: yes

Services

Telephone reference: yes
Photocopying: yes
Reading room: by appointment

Other: private counseling, group workshops, and speaker's bureau

Publications

Periodicals received: yes
Bibliographies: *Network News, International Review of Natural Family Planning.*
Finding aids/guides: *Healthful Living.*

50. THE FOUNDATION CENTER

79 Fifth Avenue
New York, New York 10003

Telephone Number

(212) 620-4230

Contact Person

Zeke Kilbride, Director, New York Library.

Objectives of Library or Information Center

To collect information about private foundations and their grant-making activities.

Access Privileges

Open to the public.

Hours

Monday, Tuesday, Thursday, Friday, 10:00–5:00; Wednesday, 10:00–8:00.

Description of Women's Materials

Information on foundations that have made or might make grants for women's issues. Includes statistics, subject indexes, program guidelines, studies, directories, periodicals, and the like.

Collection by Format

Books and monographs: yes
Pamphlets: yes
Reprints, clippings: yes

Microfiche: yes
Videotapes: 4

The most probable items of interest are the COMSEARCH printed index, "Grants for Women and Girls," and materials that will give more information about potential funding sources.

Services

Photocopying: yes
Reading room: yes
Other: weekly orientations

FRANCES HALL BALLARD LIBRARY

see Manhattan School of Music

51. FRANKLIN D. ROOSEVELT LIBRARY

259 Albany Post Road
Hyde Park, New York 12538

Telephone Number

(914) 229-8115

Contact Person

Sheryl Griffith, Librarian.

Objectives of Library or Information Center

To provide information on Franklin and Eleanor Roosevelt and their associates.

Access Privileges

Open to qualified researchers upon application.

Hours

Monday through Friday, 9:00–4:45 (except holidays).

Description of Women's Materials

There are thirty-one manuscript collections relating to women at the Franklin D. Roosevelt Library. These include the Papers of Eleanor Roosevelt, the Eleanor Roosevelt Oral History Transcripts (containing interviews with, among others, Helen Gahagan Douglas, Martha Gellhorn, Pauli Murray, Justine Wise Polier, and Marietta Tree), and materials on Mary Lasker, Frances Perkins, Hilda Smith, Caroline Ware, the Women's Division of the National Committee of the Democratic Party, and others associated with the Roosevelt administrations or with the colleagues and family of Franklin and Eleanor Roosevelt.

Collection by Format

Books and monographs: 3,000	Films: yes
Government documents: yes	Slides: 30
Pamphlets: yes	Oral history: 72
Reprints, clippings: yes	Photographs: ca. 30,000
Microfiche: yes	Manuscripts or archives: 1,555 feet
Audiotapes: yes	

The Eleanor Roosevelt Book Collection is of special interest.

Services

Telephone reference: yes
Photocopying: yes
Interlibrary loan: limited

Reading room: yes
Audiovisual facilities: yes

Publications

Finding aids/guides: *Historical Materials in the Franklin D. Roosevelt Library* (1985) lists the holdings of the Library. There are finding aids for each collection. The Registration Book, available in the Search Room, provides basic information about each collection, including biographical data on the individual who collected the papers, a brief description of the papers, restrictions on access, and information on literary property rights. Most of the larger collections have more detailed finding aids, the most common being a shelf list that indicates by folder or box the organization of the papers.

52. FRENCH INSTITUTE/ALLIANCE FRANCAISE LIBRARY

22 East 60 Street
New York, New York 10022

Telephone Number

(212) 355-6100, ext. 215

Contact Person

Fred J. Gitner, Library Director.

Objectives of Library or Information Center

To provide information on all aspects of French language, culture, and literature.

Access Privileges

Open to public for research and reference; members may borrow materials. METRO referral card honored for on-site use. Membership fee: $28.00 per year.

Hours

Monday through Thursday, 10:00–8:00; Friday, 10:00–6:00; Saturday, 10:00–1:30 (summer hours vary).

Description of Women's Materials

Resources on history, literature, and sociology of women in France and French-speaking countries. Includes bibliographies and other reference tools as well.

Collection by Format

Books and monographs: ca. 200
Audiotapes: yes

Services

Borrowing privileges: for members
Telephone reference: yes
Photocopying: yes
Interlibrary loan: yes
Reading room: yes
Audiovisual facilities: for members

Publications

Accession lists (included in general quarterly accession list).

53. GENERAL THEOLOGICAL SEMINARY

St. Mark's Library
175 Ninth Avenue
New York, New York 10011

Telephone Number

(212) 243-5150, ext. 284

Contact Person

Clifford Urr, Reference Librarian; Kim Mislin, Episcopal Women's History Project (ext. 215).

Objectives of Library or Information Center

To serve the staff, faculty, and students of the General Theological Seminary, the New York Theological Seminary, and other members of the New York Area Theological Library Association.

Access Privileges

Open to researchers with letter of reference from a faculty member of an accredited school or from an Episcopal priest. METRO referral card honored. Fees: for borrowing materials.

Hours

September through May: Monday through Thursday, 8:30 A.M.–11:30 P.M.; Friday, 8:30–5:00. Call for weekend and summer hours.

Description of Women's Materials

There is a strong reference and circulation collection on all aspects of women and religion, feminist theology, and the like. It is particularly strong in women/feminism and the Episcopal Church and Episcopal theological materials.

Collection by Format

Books and monographs: yes
Current serial titles: yes
Pamphlets: yes
Microfilm reels: yes

Microfiche: yes
Audiotapes: yes
Videotapes: yes
Manuscripts or archives: yes

The Library also houses materials for the Episcopal Women's History Project, which seeks to encourage researchers to do oral histories and other projects documenting the work of Episcopal women.

Services

Borrowing privileges: yes
Telephone reference: yes

Photocopying: yes
Interlibrary loan: yes

Publications

The Episcopal Women's History Project issues the *EWHP Newsletter.*

54. GEORGE MERCER JR. SCHOOL OF THEOLOGY LIBRARY

65 Fourth Street
Garden City, New York 11530

Telephone Number

(516) 248-4800, ext. 73

Contact Person

Wilma M. Cope, Librarian.

Objectives of Library or Information Center

To support the School of Theology curriculum and to provide service to the diocese of Long Island.

Access Privileges

Open to the public for in-house use. Borrowing privileges require approval.

Hours

Monday and Saturday, 9:00–3:00; Tuesday and Thursday, 4:00–10:00; June, July, and August, Monday only.

Description of Women's Materials

The number of items is small, but the focus is on the role of women in religion, historically, and in the present, the role of women in the clergy and as clergy wives and church women. Many of the religious serials in the collection include articles on women in religion.

Collection by Format

Books and monographs: 85
Current serial titles: 6

Services

Photocopying: yes
Interlibrary loan: yes

Reading room: yes
Audiovisual facilities: yes

Publications

Finding aids/guides: *Religion Index I, Catholic Periodicals Index*, and other general indexes.

GILL LIBRARY

see College of New Rochelle

55. GIRL SCOUTS OF THE UNITED STATES OF AMERICA ARCHIVES RESEARCH

830 Third Avenue
New York, New York 10022

Telephone Number

(212) 940-7396

Contact Person

Juana Alers-Quinones, Administrator, Library and Archives; Linda R. Laughlin, Director, Research.

Objectives of Library or Information Center

To acquire and maintain a historical record of Girl Scouting in the United States as reflected through the organizational records of the national organization, Girl Scouts of the United States of America (G.S.U.S.A.), and the G.S.U.S.A.'s National Board of Directors.

Access Privileges

Open to outside researchers upon approved request.

Hours

Monday through Friday, 9:00–4:00.

Description of Women's Materials

Collection provides seventy-five-year history (since 1912) of largest girl membership organization in the world, part of a World Association of one hundred twenty-four delegate countries. History is provided through primary sources—organizational records, publications, memorabilia, uniforms, photographs, posters, etc. Major subjects of interest include informal education (for girls), feminist history, women and volunteerism, multidimensional activities for girls, women in management, leadership training, and pluralism.

Collection by Format

Books and monographs: yes
Pamphlets: yes
Reprints, clippings: yes
Filmstrips: yes

Slides: yes
Oral history: yes
Manuscripts or archives: yes

All of the above are a part of the Archives.

Services

Photocopying: yes
Reading room: yes
Other: loans for special exhibits

Additional Information

Girl Scouts of the United States of America is preparing to enhance its Archives by taking special preservation measures and updating the collection index, thereby insuring continued historical value and access.

●

GLORIA GAINES MEMORIAL LIBRARY

see Marymount College

56. GOETHE HOUSE LIBRARY

1014 Fifth Avenue
New York, New York 10028

Telephone Number

(212) 744-8310, ext. 224

Contact Person

Gesine Worm, Head Librarian.

Objectives of Library or Information Center

To provide information on the West German cultural scene, modern German literature, contemporary history, philosophy, and the arts.

Access Privileges

Open to the public. METRO referral card honored.

Hours

Tuesday and Thursday, 12:00–7:00; Wednesday, Friday, Saturday, 12:00–5:00.

Description of Women's Materials

The collection includes books on the German women's movement and on women's role in West German society, as well as literature by women. There are feminist periodicals, *Emma, Feministische Studien,* and *Frauen und Film.*

Collection by Format

Books and monographs: yes (limited)   Reprints, clippings: yes
Current serial titles: yes   Videotapes: yes
Pamphlets: yes

There is a special collection of clippings on German film and filmmakers that is not housed in the Library, and appointments must be made to see this material.

Services

Borrowing privileges: yes   Interlibrary loan: yes
Telephone reference: yes   Reading room: yes
Photocopying: yes   Audiovisual facilities: yes

Publications

Accession lists: occasional

THE GRADUATE SCHOOL AND UNIVERSITY CENTER

see The City University of New York,
The Graduate School and University Center

●

GUSTAVE L. AND JANET W. LEVY LIBRARY

see Mount Sinai Medical Center

57. HADASSAH ARCHIVES

50 West 58 Street
New York, New York 10019

Telephone Number

(212) 303-8005

Contact Person

Lawrence Geller.

Objectives of Library or Information Center

To preserve and make available to qualified researchers the archives of the Women's Zionist Organization of America. Also to provide in-house reference assistance.

Access Privileges

Open to qualified researchers as determined by the staff and the administration.

Hours

Monday through Friday, 9:00–12:00, 1:00–5:00.

Description of Women's Materials

The Archives contain resources on women and American Zionism, child rescue in Europe during the Nazi era, women volunteerism in America, and women and Zionist education. Of special interest is the manuscript collection, the Henrietta Szold Papers in the Hadassah Archives.

Collection by Format

Microfilm reels: yes
Films: yes
Oral history: yes

Manuscripts or archives: 50 feet
Other: photographs

Services

Photocopying: yes
Reading room: yes

Publications

Finding aids/guides: Henrietta Szold Papers, Denise Tourover Ezekiel Papers, The Archives of Youth Aliyah.

Additional Information

The Hadassah Archives include an extensive collection of historical photographs documenting Hadassah's history.

●

58. HEALTH POLICY ADVISORY CENTER
17 Murray Street
New York, New York 10007

Telephone Number

(212) 267-8890

Contact Person

David Steinhardt.

Objectives of Library or Information Center

Health/PAC is a source of health policy analysis. The Women and Health Work Group publishes analyses of special interest to women in the journal, *The Health/Pac Bulletin.*

Access Privileges

Mostly by mail, but please telephone if you wish to visit.

Description of Women's Materials

The Center publishes the "Know Your Body" series of women's health booklets (a feminist approach to health pamphlets). In the *Bulletin* are articles on the impact of government health policy on the health of women.

59. THE HENRY GEORGE SCHOOL OF SOCIAL SCIENCE

Henry George Research Library
5 East 44 Street
New York, New York 10017

Telephone Number

(212) 697-9880

Contact Person

Mark A. Sullivan, Librarian.

Access Privileges

Open to the public by appointment.

Hours

Afternoons.

Description of Women's Materials

The Library has some material dealing with women's issues and economics. There is also material on the women supporters of Henry George, such as Suzanne LaFollette.

Collection by Format

Books and monographs: yes

Publications

There are numerous materials available to high school social studies teachers to heighten economic awareness among young people.

Additional Information

For more than fifty years, the Henry George School has offered free adult classes in economics and social problems. Founded in New York City by Oscar H. Geiger, the School was chartered by the Board of Regents of the University of the State of New York in 1932 and has since established branches throughout North America. Students explore such topics as world hunger, foreign trade, urban studies, city finances, property taxation, poverty, and the philosophy of Henry George.

60. THE HISPANIC SOCIETY OF AMERICA LIBRARY

Broadway between 155 and 156 Streets
New York, New York 10032

Telephone Number

(212) 926-2234

Contact Person

Gerald J. MacDonald.

Objectives of Library or Information Center

To serve as a research library for the study of Hispanic culture.

Access Privileges

Open to the public.

Hours

Tuesday through Friday, 1:00–4:30; Saturday, 10:00–4:30.

Description of Women's Materials

The collection includes materials on Hispanic women poets, writers, artists, leaders, and the like.

Services

Telephone reference: yes
Reading room: yes

This is a noncirculating library. Interlibrary loan is not available. There is no photocopying service.

Publications

Bibliographies: Early printed books; manuscripts; plays
Finding aids/guides: Card catalog

Additional Information

The Society also maintains a museum, iconography collection, sales desk, and publications list.

61. HOFSTRA UNIVERSITY LIBRARY

1000 Fulton Avenue
Hempstead, New York 11550

Telephone Number

(516) 560-5962 reference; 560-5940 administration; 560-5945 collection development

Contact Person

Vivian Wood, Collection Development Librarian.

Objectives of Library or Information Center

The Hofstra University Library supports the study and research needs of the students and faculty. Founded in 1935, the University is a private, nonsectarian, coeducational institution with 11,000 students. Eighty percent of the courses are undergraduate level, with masters programs in twenty-four liberal arts and education areas. There are doctoral programs in psychology and education.

Access Privileges

Physical access to all except during times of heavy demand by Hofstra users. Restrictions occur usually during the middle of the fall and spring semesters. Hofstra students, faculty, and members of the Cultural Center may charge out books. Additional groups with borrowing privileges include holders of Special Users Cards, including full-time faculty of reciprocating institutions, members of the Long Island Studies Institute, the Hofstra Advisory Board, Hofstra Alumni, auditing students, specific Continuing Education students, and referrals through the Long Island Research Loan Program. Fees for computerized database searches.

Hours

Open extensive hours; call 560-5967 for current schedule.

Description of Women's Materials

A collection of monographs, serials, government documents, and reference materials. Monographs relevant to women's studies are integrated within the Library of Congress classification system for the collection. Nonprint media are available at the Media Services Department, Memorial Hall, with arrangements for viewing made by faculty. Curriculum materials on the elementary and high school levels are housed in the Curriculum Materials Center, third floor. Specialized bibliographies on women are part of the reference collection.

Collection by Format

Books and monographs: yes
Current serial titles: yes
Government documents: yes
Pamphlets: yes
Reprints: in monographic form

Videotapes: yes
Films: yes
Filmstrips: yes
Slides: yes
Manuscripts or archives: yes

The Special Collections Department, housed on the ninth floor of the Library, contains manuscripts, books, and documents by and about Virginia Woolf, Vanessa Bell, Vita Sackville-West, Dora Carrington, Lady Ottline Morrell, Lydia Marie Child, and Fanny Kembel.

Services

Borrowing privileges: for Hofstra
    users
Interlibrary loan: yes
Reading room: yes

Audiovisual facilities: Memorial Hall
Photocopying: yes (restrictions on
    photocopying Special Collections
    material)

Publications

Monthly acquisitions list for all new publications.
Accession lists: yes
Bibliographies: Exhibition catalogs: *Literature and Twentieth-Century Women Writers, Eighteenth-Century Literary and Artistic Women.*
Finding aids/guides: Reference bibliographies on Women's Studies: *Women's Studies I* and *Women's Studies II.*

Additional Information

The University offers a certificate in women's studies. The Women's Studies Program was founded by Dr. Natalie Naylor and offers courses in sciences, natural sciences, women in cross-cultural studies, women's roles in society, and women's issues. The Women's Studies Program issues a newsletter and publishes a calendar.

62. HOLLAND SOCIETY OF NEW YORK LIBRARY

122 East 58 Street
New York, New York 10022

Telephone Number

(212) 758-1871

Contact Person

Robin Siegel.

Objectives of Library or Information Center

To collect information on New Netherland—seventeenth and eighteenth centuries.

Access Privileges

Open to the public on Friday. $2.00 donation requested.

Hours

Friday, 11:00–4:00.

Description of Women's Materials

Some scattered books and vertical file materials on the women of New Netherland. Not extensive and not all in one place. Also individual biographical materials on specific seventeenth- and eighteenth-century women.

Collection by Format

Books and monographs: some
Reprints, clippings: some

Services

Telephone reference: yes
Photocopying: yes
Reading room: yes

63. HUNTER COLLEGE OF THE CITY UNIVERSITY OF NEW YORK LIBRARY

695 Park Avenue
New York, New York 10021

Telephone Number

(212) 772-4146

Objectives of Library or Information Center

The collection supports the curriculum of the Women's Studies Program. It is housed in the Wexler Library and the School of Social Work Library.

Access Privileges

Open to CUNY students, faculty, and staff. METRO referral card honored.

Hours

Monday through Thursday, 9:00–9:00; Friday, 9:00–5:00; Saturday, 10:00–5:00.

Description of Women's Materials

This is a broad collection that supports the Women's Studies Program at Hunter and is interdisciplinary. While the collection is relatively strong, there are no particular areas that are especially outstanding.

Services

Borrowing privileges: for members of CUNY
Interlibrary loan: yes

64. HUNTINGTON FREE LIBRARY/MUSEUM OF THE AMERICAN INDIAN LIBRARY

9 Westchester Square
Bronx, New York 10461

Telephone Number

(212) 829-7770

Contact Person

Mary B. Davis.

Objectives of Library or Information Center

To be a research library on native peoples of the Western Hemisphere.

Access Privileges

Open to the public by appointment. METRO referral card honored.

Hours

Monday through Friday, 10:00–4:30; also open first and third Saturdays of each month.

Description of Women's Materials

The collection includes materials on native American women from North, Middle, and South America. It also includes the Papers of the Women's National Indian Association. With a few exceptions, the resources on Indian women are integrated into the rest of the collection; there is not a separate women's collection.

Collection by Format

Books and monographs: yes
Current serial titles: yes
Government documents: yes
Pamphlets: yes

Reprints, clippings: yes
Microfilm reels: yes
Manuscripts or archives: yes

Services

Telephone reference: yes
Photocopying: yes
Reading room: yes

Publications

Finding aids/guides: *Dictionary Catalog of the American Indian.*

Additional Information

One of the leading research sources on Indians of the Western Hemisphere, the Museum Library Collection contains materials on the archaeology, ethnology, and history of the native peoples of the Americas, as well as on current native American affairs and Indian biography.

65. THE HUNTINGTON HISTORICAL SOCIETY

209 Main Street
Huntington, New York 11743

Telephone Number

(516) 427-7045

Contact Person

Gay Wagner, Director, Huntington Historical Society; Irene Sniffin, Library Registrar.

Objectives of Library or Information Center

To acquire and preserve research and documentary material on the local history, social history, and the material culture of Huntington, central Long Island, New York, and southern New England as a support to the work of the museum.

Access Privileges

Open to the public. Fees: $1.00 per day (for nonmembers).

Hours

Tuesday through Saturday, 10:00–4:00.

Description of Women's Materials

The general collections contain considerable primary material on women in the Huntington community and women in families.

Collection by Format

Books and monographs: yes
Pamphlets: yes
Reprints, clippings: yes
Microfilm reels: yes

Slides: yes
Oral history: yes
Manuscripts or archives: yes

There are strong family history collections. The local history materials include nineteenth- and twentieth-century county and regional histories and history tapes and transcripts, newspapers (including *The Long Islander*, dating from 1839), maps and atlases, and scrapbooks. There is also an extensive collection of photographs and slides. The genealogy vertical file collection is similarly extensive.

Services

Borrowing privileges: noncirculating   Reading room: yes
Photocopying: yes   Audiovisual facilities: yes

Publications

The Society's publications include thirteen titles, a monthly newsletter for members, and the *Quarterly,* a journal of scholarly articles on history, genealogy, and the decorative arts. Finding aids are being developed for the manuscript materials. The principal newspaper, *The Long Islander,* is indexed (1839–1860). The positive photographs are filed by category, and an indexing project is underway to make the copy negatives easier to use. Many photographs and documents are available in slide form and are indexed.

66. THE INSTITUTE FOR RESEARCH IN HISTORY

The Margaret Sanger Papers
1133 Broadway, Suite 923
New York, New York 10012

Telephone Number

(212) 691-7316

Contact Person

Esther Katz, Director.

Objectives of Library or Information Center

To locate, collect, and publish the public and private papers of Margaret Sanger. A comprehensive microfilm edition and a selected four-volume book edition are being planned.

Access Privileges

Open to scholars on a limited basis.

Hours

By appointment.

Description of Women's Materials

The papers document the life and work of Margaret Sanger and the development of the birth control movement in the twentieth century. Subjects covered include sex roles, physical health, and the history of the feminist and reform movements.

Collection by Format

Pamphlets: yes
Manuscripts or archives: yes (some 300 documents at present, but growing quickly)

Services

Telephone reference: yes

Publications

Finding aids/guides: forthcoming

INSTITUTE OF JAZZ STUDIES

see Rutgers, The State University of New Jersey

67. INTERNATIONAL WOMEN'S TRIBUNE CENTRE

777 UN Plaza (12th Floor)
New York, New York 10017

Telephone Number

(212) 687-8633

Contact Person

Lucy A. Peipins, Resource Centre Coordinator.

Objectives of Library or Information Center

To identify and collect materials useful to the planning and implementation of women-oriented development programs; to develop subject-specific bibliographies for use in International Women's Tribune Centre publications; to develop and maintain reference collections in areas related to women and development.

Access Privileges

Open to the public by appointment. METRO referral card honored.

Hours

By appointment.

Description of Women's Materials

The Centre serves as a clearinghouse of information on women's issues in Third World countries and houses a comprehensive collection of documents and resource materials covering a wide spectrum of development issues.

Collection by Format

Books and monographs: ca. 4,000   Reprints, clippings: yes
Current serial titles: ca. 600   Slides: ca. 9,000
Pamphlets: yes

Collection contains seventy-two drawers of unpublished and published papers, reports, studies, project data, training materials, and organizational information. Special reference tools and/or special collections:

Organizational Data Bank: Notebooks containing organizational profiles of women's organizations and development organizations with special reference to the organization's projects, publications, and resource people.

Slide Collection: Slides from every region of the world depict women in their daily lives, in rural and urban areas, with special emphasis on women engaged in nontraditional roles and activities.

Educational Media: Collection of training materials from around the world that can be produced locally at low cost.

Poster and Button Collection: Women's posters and buttons collected from around the world.

Non-Governmental Women's Conferences Archives: Documents from the 1975 International Women's Year Tribune, and 1980 and 1985 Forums (non-governmental world conferences).

Services

Telephone reference: yes   Reading room: yes
Photocopying: yes   Audiovisual facilities: slide projectors

Publications

The Centre publishes a variety of publications that include a quarterly journal on women and development, *The Tribune,* in English, French, and Spanish; annotated bibliographies on specific issues; and training manuals. *The Tribune* is directed primarily at Third World women involved in development projects and provides information on projects and resources, as well as on United Nations' and other development organizations' activities. Back issues have focused on women, marketing, and small industries; rural women; women and appropriate technology; women and food production; women's networks; women and media; women, money, and credit; women and water; women and training activities; peace as a women's issue; and women and funds.

●

IRENE LEWISOHN COSTUME REFERENCE LIBRARY

see The Metropolitan Museum of Art

68. ITALIAN CULTURAL INSTITUTE

686 Park Avenue
New York, New York 10021

Telephone Number

(212) 879-4242

Contact Person

Maria Gargotta.

Objectives of Library or Information Center

The collection contains only matters of Italian interest.

Access Privileges

Open to the public. $10.00 deposit for library card (for books).

Hours

Monday through Friday, 9:00–1:00, 2:00–5:00.

Description of Women's Materials

Contains a small number of books in Italian on women in Italy.

Collection by Format

Books and monographs: yes

Services

Borrowing privileges: yes   Interlibrary loan: yes
Photocopying: yes   Reading room: yes

69. JERSEY CITY STATE COLLEGE WOMEN'S CENTER

Jersey City, New Jersey 07305

Telephone Number

(201) 547-3189

Contact Person

Harriet Alonso.

Objectives of Library or Information Center

To provide archives for anyone interested in specific topics concerning women; to provide reference for those in need.

Access Privileges

Open to the public.

Hours

Monday through Friday, 8:30–4:30, and by appointment.

Description of Women's Materials

The holdings range through a wide variety of women's issues. There are also clipping and referral files.

Collection by Format

Books and monographs: ca. 100
Reprints, clippings: thousands
Pamphlets: hundreds

Services

Borrowing privileges: yes
Reading room: yes
Telephone reference: yes

70. JEWISH THEOLOGICAL SEMINARY OF AMERICA

Library
3080 Broadway
New York, New York 10027-4649

Telephone Number

(212) 678-8081/8982

Contact Person

Dvorah Savitzky, Circulation Librarian.

Objectives of Library or Information Center

The Library contains one of the largest and most exhaustive collections of Hebraica and Judaica in the world. It is rich in primary sources for research in the Bible and its Jewish commentaries, rabbinics, Jewish philosophy, liturgy, history, and medieval and modern Hebrew literature.

Access Privileges

Open to the public for on-site use.

Hours

Academic year: Monday through Thursday, 8:00 A.M.–10:00 P.M.; Friday, 8:00–5:00; Sunday, 9:30 A.M.–10:00 P.M. Recess: Monday through Friday, 8:30–5:00.

Description of Women's Materials

The Library has biographies of Jewish women and materials on the history of Jewish women, the legal status and laws with regard to Jewish women, literary collections, information on women and Judaism, on women and religion, on women in the Bible and Talmud, and on women in Israel.

Collection by Format

Books and monographs: 600
Current serial titles: 4

Services

Borrowing privileges: members only
Telephone reference: yes
Photocopying: yes
Interlibrary loan: yes

Reading room: yes
Audiovisual facilities: microform center

JEWISH WOMEN'S RESOURCE CENTER

see National Council of Jewish Women

•

KATHARINE DEXTER McCORMICK LIBRARY

see Planned Parenthood Federation of America, Inc.

71. KINGSBOROUGH COMMUNITY COLLEGE

Robert J. Kibbee Library
2001 Oriental Boulevard
Brooklyn, New York 11235

Telephone Number

(718) 934-5632

Contact Person

Florence Houser.

Objectives of Library or Information Center

To support the various curricula of the College; to meet the information needs of students, faculty, and staff; and to assist faculty in the area of scholarly research.

Access Privileges

Open to Kingsborough's students, faculty, and staff; City University of New York faculty and students have open access; other outside users have on-site access. METRO referral card honored.

Hours

Monday through Thursday, 8:30 A.M.–9:00 P.M.; Friday, 8:30–5:00; Saturday, 10:00–3:00 (fall and spring semesters only).

Description of Women's Materials

Resources on careers of working women; the history of women (antiquity, reformers, etc.). Also includes biographical material on the country's first ladies; materials on the status of women in many countries and regions; the social problems of women; sex roles; folklore and mythology of women.

Collection by Format

Books and monographs: ca. 1,800
Current serial titles: 28
Audiotapes: 2
Films: 9
Filmstrips: 1 set of 4
Pamphlets: ca. 300 (about 50 subject headings)

Services

Telephone reference: yes
Photocopying: yes
Audiovisual facilities: yes
Reading room: yes
Interlibrary loan: yes

Publications

Bibliographies: *Women's History Month: A Filmography.*

●

LANE, BETTYE

see Bettye Lane

72. LEO BAECK INSTITUTE

129 East 73 Street
New York, New York 10021

Telephone Number

(212) 744-6400

Contact Person

Diane Spielmann, Archivist; Jacqueline Graf, Librarian.

Objectives of Library or Information Center

To be a research center for the history of German-speaking Jewry of Central Europe from the Enlightenment through the Holocaust.

Access Privileges

Open to the public, with special privileges for members (mailings, lectures).

Hours

Monday through Thursday, 9:00–5:00; Friday, 9:00–3:00.

Description of Women's Materials

The Institute collection contains works relating to German-Jewish women. The archival collection includes ample material on various Jewish women's organizations that existed before the Holocaust, such as "Juedischer Frauenbund, Bertha Pappenheim." It also includes many collections on professional women, e.g., social workers and physicians, memoirs by professional women and wives of professionals, and the like.

Collection by Format

Books and monographs: yes
Archives: yes

Services

Telephone reference: limited
Photocopying: yes

Interlibrary loan: yes
Reading room: yes

Publications

Bibliographies: Subject listings on women integrated within references in archival card catalog.
Finding aids/guides: Card catalog, inventories; printed catalog for archival holdings forthcoming.

Additional Information

The fifty-thousand volume library of the Institute is recognized as the foremost reference source in its field. Rich in rarities ranging from early sixteenth-century writings to Moses Mendelssohn first editions and dedication copies of works of prominent writers of recent generations, many of its volumes were salvaged from famous Jewish libraries destroyed by the Nazis. The library includes a comprehensive collection of belles lettres written by Jews, extensive material on the "Jewish Problem" and on anti-Semitism, and more than seven hundred fifty periodicals published by Jews from the eighteenth to twentieth centuries. The archives contain thousands of family, business, institutional, and community records that touch upon virtually every phase of German-Jewish life during the past two hundred years. Materials relate not only to famous women and men of the past but also to the life of the average Jewish person.

73. LESBIAN HERSTORY EDUCATIONAL FOUNDATION, INC./LESBIAN HERSTORY ARCHIVES

P.O. Box 1258
New York, New York 10116

Telephone Number

(212) 874-7232

Contact Person

Deborah Edel.

Objectives of Library or Information Center

To collect, preserve, and make available all aspects of lesbian life and culture.

Access Privileges

Open by appointment.

Hours

By appointment.

Description of Women's Materials

The collection contains material on all aspects of lesbian culture.

Collection by Format

Books and monographs: 8,000	Films: yes
Pamphlets: thousands	Slides: yes
Reprints, clippings: thousands	Oral history: yes
Audiotapes: yes	Manuscripts or archives: large collection
Videotapes: yes	

Services

Telephone reference: yes	Audiovisual facilities: yes
Photocopying: yes	Other: slide shows, public speaking
Reading room: yes	

Publications

Bibliographies, Finding aids/guides: *Lesbian Herstory Archives News;* occasional bibliographies.

MABEL SMITH DOUGLASS LIBRARY

see Rutgers, The State University of New Jersey

74. MANHASSET PUBLIC LIBRARY

Thirty Onderdonk Avenue
Manhasset, New York 11030

Telephone Number

(516) 627-2300

Contact Person

Florine Polner.

Objectives of Library or Information Center

The Manhasset Local History collection is a collection of books, documents, photographs, and the like, illustrating the history of Manhasset.

Access Privileges

Open to the public for in-house use.

Hours

September through May: Monday through Thursday, 9:00–9:00 (11:00–9:00 on Tuesday); Friday, Saturday, 9:00–5:30; Sunday, 12:00–4:30.

Description of Women's Materials

There are biographical materials, books, and pictures of Frances Hodgson Burnett, who was a Manhasset author. There are many first editions of her books and reproductions of her correspondence with Scribner's, her publisher. There is also an original of the copybook of Louisa Udall, a schoolgirl who attended school in Manhasset during the 1850s.

Services

Borrowing privileges: residents only
Telephone reference: yes
Reading room: yes

75. MANHATTAN SCHOOL OF MUSIC

Frances Hall Ballard Library
120 Claremont Avenue
New York, New York 10027

Telephone Number

(212) 749-2802, ext. 511

Contact Person

Richard Presser, Reference Librarian.

Objectives of Library or Information Center

To serve as curriculum support for the music conservatory in order to meet classroom instruction and performing needs.

Access Privileges

Open for on-site use on space-available basis. METRO referral card honored.

Hours

Monday through Thursday, 9:00–9:00; Friday, 9:00–6:00; summer, Monday through Thursday, 9:00–6:00.

Description of Women's Materials

The Library contains music scores and recordings by women composers and performers, as well as biographical materials on women musicians.

Collection by Format

Books and monographs: yes
Audiotapes: yes
Other: sound recordings

There is a set of selected works of S.C. Eckhardt-Gramatte.

Services

Photocopying: yes   Reading room: yes
Interlibrary loan: yes   Audio facilities: yes

76. MANHATTANVILLE COLLEGE LIBRARY

Purchase, New York 10577

Telephone Number

(914) 694-2200, ext. 282

Contact Person

Stefania Koren.

Objectives of Library or Information Center

To support an undergraduate liberal arts college.

Access Privileges

Open to students and the public (no borrowing privileges for the public). METRO referral card honored.

Hours

Monday through Friday, 8:30 A.M.–11:00 P.M.; Saturday, 11:00–11:00 during fall and spring semesters.

Description of Women's Materials

There are no special monograph collections on women's materials, but the archival materials may be of some interest. Manhattanville College was founded by the Roman Catholic women's religious community, Society of the Sacred Heart, in 1841, as a college for women. It became coeducational in the early 1970s and is no longer a Catholic college, but its archives would be of interest to serious scholars in the areas of women's religious orders, higher education of women, women's colleges in the United States, etc.

Collection by Format

Manuscripts or archives: yes

Services

Telephone reference: limited   Reading room: yes
Photocopying: yes   Audiovisual facilities: yes
Interlibrary loan: yes

Additional Information

Currently, Manhattanville does not have an archivist and, therefore, the resources of the archives are not easily available except via prior arrangement through the Office of the Library Director.

MARY S. CALDERONE LIBRARY

see Sex Information and Education Council of the United States

77. MARYKNOLL SCHOOL OF THEOLOGY LIBRARY

Maryknoll, New York 10545

Telephone Number

(914) 941-7590, ext. 427

Contact Person

Reverend Arthur Brown, Librarian.

Objectives of Library or Information Center

To serve the research needs of the Catholic Foreign Mission Society of America and the students of the Maryknoll School of Theology.

Access Privileges

Open to all, with special permission of the Librarian. METRO referral card honored.

Hours

Monday through Friday, 8:30–4:00.

Description of Women's Materials

Materials on women in developing countries, women and religion, and women in Christianity.

Collection by Format

Books and monographs: 800

Services

Telephone reference: yes   Interlibrary loan: yes
Photocopying: yes   Reading room: yes

78. MARYMOUNT COLLEGE

Gloria Gaines Memorial Library
Tarrytown, New York 10591

Telephone Number

(914) 631-3200, ext. 251

Contact Person

Sister Virginia McKenna, Library Director.

Objectives of Library or Information Center

To provide the best possible service to the entire Marymount community, to assist the faculty and students in their courses, and to strengthen the Library collection in all areas relating to the curriculum.

Access Privileges

Open to adults for on-site use. METRO referral card honored.

Hours

During academic semester: Monday through Thursday, 8:15 A.M.–11:00 P.M.; Friday, 8:15 A.M.–10:00 P.M.; Saturday, 9:00–9:00; Sunday, 9:00 A.M.–11:00 P.M.

Description of Women's Materials

There is a basic collection on women authors, history, literature, psychology, sociology, and the like. There are also a number of good bibliographies.

Collection by Format

Books and monographs: ca. 3,000
Current serial titles: ca. 12

The Library contains the series, *American Women: Images and Realities*, an Arno Press collection of about forty-four titles.

Services

Borrowing privileges: yes   Photocopying: yes
Telephone reference: yes   Interlibrary loan: yes

79. MARYMOUNT MANHATTAN COLLEGE

Thomas J. Shanahan Library
221 East 71 Street
New York, New York 10021

Telephone Number

(212) 517-0460; 517-0590

Objectives of Library or Information Center

To meet the needs of students, faculty, and the administration of Marymount Manhattan College, an undergraduate liberal arts college for women.

Access Privileges

Open to Friends of the Library; selected high schools; Mannes College of Music; Malcolm-King: Harlem College Extension; open to others upon request to the Head Librarian. METRO referral card honored. Fees: Friends of the Library membership, $35.00, family membership, $45.00.

Hours

Monday through Thursday, 9:00–8:00; Friday, 9:00–7:00; Saturday, 10:00–4:00; Sunday, 12:00–5:00.

Description of Women's Materials

The collection includes a basic core of materials on women's studies in general, as well as on women and work, women and literature, women and politics, and the like.

Collection by Format

Books and monographs: ca. 2,000
Current serial titles: 20
Government documents: yes
Pamphlets: yes

Audiotapes: ca. 75
Videotapes: 3
Manuscripts or archives: yes

The Library contains the Geraldine A. Ferraro Papers, a repository of legislative and campaign correspondence, legislative materials, speeches, *Congressional Record* statements, cosponsored bills, press releases, press clippings, audio and video cassettes, photographs, and memorabilia that document the congresswoman's work in Congress from 1979 through 1984 and the 1984 vice-presidential campaign. The Ferraro Papers, which were acquired in 1986, are currently being inventoried, and access has not yet been determined.

Services

Borrowing privileges: Friends of the
    Library
Telephone reference: yes
Photocopying: yes

Interlibrary loan: yes
Reading room: yes
Audiovisual facilities: yes

Publications

Periodical Holdings on Women's Studies.

80. MATERNITY CENTER ASSOCIATION LIBRARY

48 East 92 Street
New York, New York 10128

Telephone Number

(212) 369-7300

Contact Person

Librarian.

Objectives of Library or Information Center

The Maternity Center Association is a national nonprofit health agency dedicated to the improvement of maternity and infant care.

Access Privileges

Open to the public; call for an appointment.

Hours

Monday through Friday, 9:00–5:00.

Description of Women's Materials

Includes resources on maternal and child health, preparation for childbearing, prenatal and postnatal care, nurse-midwifery, obstetrics, family life, education for parenthood, nutrition, child care, and public health.

Collection by Format

Books and monographs: 2,450
Current serial titles: 45

Services

Telephone reference: yes
Reading room: yes
Photocopying: yes

81. MEDGAR EVERS COLLEGE

Center for Women's Development
1150 Carroll Street
Brooklyn, New York 11225

Telephone Number

(718) 735-1903

Contact Person

Safiya Bandele, Director.

Objectives of Library or Information Center

The Center for Women's Development provides counseling, advocacy, and referral services. A mini-library is available for research information on a range of women's issues and women's services.

Access Privileges

Open to CUNY students, faculty, and staff.

Hours

Monday through Friday, 9:00–5:00; Saturday, 10:00–1:00.

Description of Women's Materials

A special effort is made to acquire materials on women of color, particularly African and Caribbean women and black women in America. The book collection contains fiction with special emphasis on women of color. The nonfiction collection covers many areas, especially women's socialization. There are pamphlets and newsletters on Asian women, black women's health, women's studies, and women of color studies. There is a videotape of a black women's conference.

Collection by Format

Books and monographs: 250
Pamphlets: 35
Government documents: 10

Reprints, clippings: 4 files
Videotapes: 6 (hours)

Services

Borrowing privileges: requests must be negotiated
Telephone reference: requests must be negotiated

Publications

Bibliographies: *Afro-American Women: A Selected Bibliography; Women: Past and Present; A Selected Bibliography of Materials in the Collections of Medgar Evers College Library.*

82. MEDGAR EVERS COLLEGE LIBRARY

1150 Carroll Street
Brooklyn, New York 11225

Telephone Number

(718) 735-1851

Contact Person

Suzine Har Nicolescu, Chief Librarian and Chair, Library Division.

Objectives of Library or Information Center

To support the mission of Medgar Evers College.

Access Privileges

Open to Medgar Evers College students, faculty, staff; CUNY students, faculty, staff; Academic Libraries of Brooklyn members. METRO referral card honored.

Hours

Monday through Thursday, 8:30–8:00; Friday, 8:30–5:00; Saturday, 10:00–5:00.

Description of Women's Materials

The Library contains material on the psychology and health of women, the history of the role of women during the nineteenth and twentieth centuries, and women in the arts.

Collection by Format

Books and monographs: 550
Audiotapes: 40
Microfilm reels: 2

Films: 4
Filmstrips: 7
Other: 3 multimedia kits

Services

Borrowing privileges: yes
Photocopying: yes
Telephone reference: yes

Interlibrary loan: yes
Reading room: yes
Audiovisual facilities: yes

Publications

Bibliographies: *Women: Past and Present; A Selected Bibliography of Materials in the Collections of Medgar Evers College Library* (1985).
Finding aids/guides: Subject catalog file with entries for women.

83. MERCY COLLEGE LIBRARIES

555 Broadway
Dobbs Ferry, New York 10522

Telephone Number

(914) 693-4500, ext. 257

Contact Person

Marieta Tobey, Head, Public Services.

Objectives of Library or Information Center

To support the research efforts of Mercy College students and faculty.

Access Privileges

On-site use only for the general public. METRO referral card honored.

Hours

Monday through Thursday, 8:00 A.M.–10:30 P.M.; Friday, 8:00 A.M.–9:00 P.M.; Saturday, 9:00–5:00; Sunday, 1:00–5:00. Call for summer hours.

Description of Women's Materials

Basic college-level collection of women's materials that contains primarily monographs. Collection strengths include women and employment, feminism, and women in literature.

Collection by Format

Books and monographs: 4,000
Government documents: yes
Current serial titles: 9
Microfilm reels: 47
Microfiche: 72
Videotapes: 6

Audiotapes: 11
Films: 1
Filmstrips: 15 (sound)
Slides: 6 (sound)
Records: 5

Services

Borrowing privileges: Mercy College affiliates only
Interlibrary loan: Mercy College affiliates only

Photocopying: yes
Reading room: yes
Audiovisual facilities: yes

84. THE METROPOLITAN MUSEUM OF ART

Irene Lewisohn Costume Reference Library
Fifth Avenue at 82 Street
New York, New York 10028

Telephone Number

(212) 879-5500, ext. 3018

Contact Person

Robert C. Kaufmann, Associate Museum Librarian.

Objectives of Library or Information Center

To support the research of the Museum staff.

Access Privileges

Open to qualified adult researchers; call for an appointment.

Hours

Wednesday through Friday, 10:00–12:30 and 1:30–4:00, except holidays.

Description of Women's Materials

The collection has as its focus the history of costume, beauty, and social history. There is a great deal of information about women, but the materials are not arranged in any way that isolates the contributions by women to the history of costume and fashion or to the fashion industry. It is possible that some seventy percent of the material is concerned with women's clothing, women's beauty, and women as objects of beauty—materials on women's fashions, cosmetics, wigs, hair styles, fashion magazines, and the like.

Collection by Format

Books and monographs: yes
Current serial titles: yes
Reprints, clippings: yes

Manuscripts or archives: yes
Other: photographs, drawings, prints

Services

Photocopying: yes
Reading room: yes

85. THE METROPOLITAN MUSEUM OF ART

Thomas J. Watson Library
Fifth Avenue at 82 Street
New York, New York 10028

Telephone Number

(212) 879-5500, ext. 3221

Contact Person

William B. Walker, Chief Librarian.

Objectives of Library or Information Center

The primary objective is to support the research of the curators, educators, conservators, editors, administrators, and other researchers of the Museum staff.

Access Privileges

The Library is open to qualified adult researchers: graduate students, faculty of schools and universities, professional artists and designers, art historians, writers, collectors, and personnel of art galleries and auction houses.

Hours

Tuesday through Friday, 10:00–4:45. Closed holidays and the month of August.

Description of Women's Materials

The collections include a great deal of material on women as artists working in all media, women as the subjects of art, women collectors, women art dealers, and the like. However, much of the standard cataloging and indexing has not analyzed the involvement of women as such, and the materials are, therefore, not readily tagged as such. In addition to the cataloged volumes, the Library has extensive collections of vertical file materials, and some of the clippings and pamphlets are on women and the visual arts.

Collection by Format

Books and monographs: yes   Pamphlets: yes
Current serial titles: yes   Reprints, clippings: yes

The Thomas J. Watson Library is the central library of the Museum, and has the largest (independent) collection in the hemisphere on the art and archaeology of the world. There are substantial runs of periodicals and art museum bulletins, art auction catalogs, and art exhibition and collection catalogs, as well as the standard monographs on art in general, painting, sculpture, graphic arts, drawing, photography, architecture, and decorative arts, including thousands of volumes on individual artists who work in the various media.

Services

Photocopying: yes
Reading room: yes

●

MIDMARCH ARTS

see Women Artists News

●

MINA REES LIBRARY

see The City University of New York,
The Graduate School and University Center

86. MONMOUTH COUNTY HISTORICAL ASSOCIATION

70 Court Street
Freehold, New Jersey 07728

Telephone Number

(201) 462-1466

Contact Person

Kathleen Stavec, Librarian.

Objectives of Library or Information Center

To collect and disseminate Monmouth County history.

Access Privileges

Open to the public. $2.00 admission fee.

Hours

Wednesday through Saturday, 10:00–4:00.

Description of Women's Materials

The collection is of a general nature, but there are manuscript materials (i.e., correspondence, journals, and the like). The Freehold, New Jersey Young Ladies' Seminary Collection is of special note.

Collection by Format

Manuscripts or archives: yes

Services

Telephone reference: yes
Reading room: yes
Photocopying: yes

87. MOUNT SINAI MEDICAL CENTER

Gustave L. and Janet W. Levy Library
One Gustave L. Levy Place (100 Street and Fifth Avenue)
New York, New York 10029

Telephone Number

(212) 650-6675

Contact Person

Dorothy R. Hill, Collection Development Librarian.

Objectives of Library or Information Center

To serve the educational, research, and health care programs of the Center and the clinical practice and continuing education needs of its staff.

Access Privileges

Open to faculty and staff of the Center and its affiliates; CUNY faculty and graduate students; and by appointment with approval of the Library Director. METRO referral card honored. Fees: $6.00 per book loan and $6.00 per photo duplication request with additional charges for each increment of 25 pages or more.

Hours

Monday through Thursday, 8:00 A.M.–11:50 P.M.; Friday, 8:00 A.M.–9:50 P.M; Saturday, 10:00–8:50, during the academic year.

Description of Women's Materials

The Levy Library collection contains current sources of information, at the professional level, on the health aspects of women, such as obstetrics and gynecology. At present, the collection is being developed in the area of women and aging. The Levy Library does not contain materials for the layperson or health consumer, and its resources relating to women may not be useful for traditional research in women's studies.

Collection by Format

Books and monographs: 1,200
Current serial titles: 50
Microfiche: 4
Audiotapes: 6
Videotapes: 60

Films: 1
Slides: 50
Other: 4 computer-assisted instruction programs

Services (for authorized patrons only)

Telephone reference: yes
Photocopying: yes
Interlibrary loan: yes
Reading room: yes

Audiovisual facilities: yes
Computer facilities: yes
Database services: yes

88. MUSEUM OF MODERN ART LIBRARY

11 West 53 Street
New York, New York 10019

Telephone Number

(212) 708-9433 (reference desk)

Objectives of Library or Information Center

To document modern art from 1880 to the present.

Access Privileges

Open to researchers and the public; appointments preferred. METRO referral card honored.

Hours

Monday through Friday, 11:00–5:00.

Description of Women's Materials

The collection includes materials on painting, sculpture, drawing, prints, photography, film, video, architecture, design, artists' books, inter-media, mixed media, and the like. The material on women artists is not separately organized, but some access is provided through the card catalog.

Collection by Format

Books and monographs: yes
Current serial titles: yes
Pamphlets: yes
Microfilm reels: yes

Audiotapes: yes
Manuscripts or archives: yes
Films (artists'): yes

Information on film and video also available through the Film Study Center, and information on photography through the Photography Study Center.

Services

Telephone reference: yes
Photocopying: yes
Interlibrary loan: yes

Reading room: yes
Audiovisual facilities: limited

MUSEUM OF THE AMERICAN INDIAN LIBRARY

see Huntington Free Library

89. MUSEUM OF THE CITY OF NEW YORK

Photo Archives
Fifth Avenue at 103 Street
New York, New York 10029

Telephone Number

(212) 534-1672

Objectives of Library or Information Center

To provide a source of information and visuals on New York City history.

Access Privileges

Open to the public by appointment.

Hours

Monday through Friday, 10:00–4:30.

Description of Women's Materials

The Archives include photographs of street scenes and interior views of residences and work situations. The historical views are strongest for the period up to the 1940s.

Collection by Format

Reprints, clippings: yes
Manuscripts or archives: yes
Photographs: yes

Services

Photocopying: yes
Other: copy prints may be ordered

90. THE MUSEUMS AT STONY BROOK

1208 Route 25 A
Stony Brook, New York 11790

Telephone Number

(516) 751-0066, ext. 32

Contact Person

Lisa Royse.

Objectives of Library or Information Center

To acquire library materials relating to items in the Museum's collections.

Access Privileges

Open to the public by appointment.

Hours

Monday through Friday, 9:00–5:00.

Description of Women's Materials

There are women's costumes and a collection of oil paintings by the nineteenth-century Long Island artist, Evelina Mount.

Collection by Format

Books and monographs: 25

Services

Photocopying: yes
Reading room: yes

91. NASSAU COMMUNITY COLLEGE LIBRARY

Stewart Avenue
Garden City, New York 11530

Telephone Number

(516) 222-7408

Contact Person

Aurelia Stephan, Reference Librarian.

Objectives of Library or Information Center

To fulfill the requirements of the College's curriculum.

Access Privileges

Open to the public for on-site use.

Hours

Monday through Thursday, 8:00 A.M.–10:30 P.M.; Friday, 8:00–5:00; Saturday and Sunday, 12:00–5:00.

Description of Women's Materials

The collection is a general one, with emphasis on literature, history, and sociology. It includes Elizabeth Cady Stanton's multivolume *History of Woman Suffrage* as well as *Women's History Sources, Women Studies Abstracts,* and *Herstory* (on microfilm).

Collection by Format

Books and monographs: yes
Government documents: yes

Current serial titles: yes
Pamphlets: yes

Services

Telephone reference: yes
Audiovisual facilities: yes
Interlibrary loan: yes
Photocopying: yes

Reading room: yes
Other: class lectures, bibliographical
    instruction

Publications

Bibliographies: Prepared upon request.

92. NATIONAL ASSOCIATION FOR FEMALE EXECUTIVES

1041 Third Avenue
New York, New York 10021

Telephone Number

(212) 371-0740

Contact Person

Leslie Smith, Associate Director.

Objectives of Library or Information Center

The Association is a resource on career-related information, with special reference to networking and contacts.

Access Privileges

Open to the public by appointment.

Hours

Monday through Friday, 9:00–5:30.

Description of Women's Materials

The National Association for Female Executives does not maintain a formal library. It has a number of magazines, such as *The Executive Female*. Of note, however, are the one thousand networks that it has to refer women to each other on a national basis.

Collection by Format

Current serial titles: yes

Services

Telephone reference: yes

93. NATIONAL CENTER FOR THE STUDY OF COLLECTIVE BARGAINING IN HIGHER EDUCATION AND THE PROFESSIONS

Elias Lieberman Higher Education Contract Library
11 East 18 Street, Room 1051
New York, New York 10010

Telephone Number

(212) 725-3390

Contact Person

Beth Hillman.

Objectives of Library or Information Center

The National Center is an impartial, nonprofit educational institution serving as a clearinghouse and forum for those engaged in collective bargaining in colleges and universities. Operating on the campus of Baruch College, CUNY, it addresses its research to scholars and practitioners in the field.

Access Privileges

Open to members; open to others with special permission. METRO referral card honored.

Hours

Monday through Friday, 9:00–5:00.

Description of Women's Materials

Information on employment and promotion practices in higher education is an integral part of the collection. The Library contains more than three hundred college and university collective bargaining agreements and important books and research reports on the subject.

Collection by Format

Books and monographs: yes
Government documents: yes

The Library is an arbitration depository containing copies of all awards. A computerized retrieval system has been designed to provide data needed for collective bargaining and research purposes. Specific language and quantitative analyses are available at reduced rates for members. The system accesses the contract data bank.

Services

Telephone reference: yes
Photocopying: yes
Reading room: yes

Publications

Bibliographies: *Bibliography on Sex Discrimination, Salary, and Tenure in Higher Education Employment Practices.*

94. NATIONAL COUNCIL FOR RESEARCH ON WOMEN

Sara Delano Roosevelt Memorial House
47–49 East 65 Street
New York, New York 10021

Telephone Number

(212) 570-5001

Contact Person

Mariam K. Chamberlain, President.

Objectives of Library or Information Center

To provide a brief overview of member institutions' programs of feminist research and policy analysis, including selected publications by individual members. Currently developing an international guide to information resources on women.

Access Privileges

Written or telephone inquiry preferred. Limited public access.

Hours

Monday through Friday, 9:00–5:00.

Description of Women's Materials

As a membership organization, the bulk of the collection is comprised of member institutions' materials, including some working papers and publications. Other areas of focus include women and higher education, women and language, and women and agricultural development. Though not a library, the Council does have limited resources for preliminary research.

Collection by Format

Books and monographs: yes
Current serial titles: yes
Pamphlets: yes

Reprints, clippings: yes
Other: brochures, unpublished papers, newsletters, working papers

Services

Telephone reference: yes

Publications

Bibliographies: *Third World Women in Agriculture: An Annotated Bibliography,* by Shelly Kessler (July 1985).
Finding aids/guides: *Directory of Members, Opportunities for Research and*

Study (a listing of member centers' programs), *Women International Resource Guide* (forthcoming).

●

95. NATIONAL COUNCIL OF JEWISH WOMEN— NEW YORK SECTION

Jewish Women's Resource Center
9 East 69 Street
New York, New York 10021

Telephone Number

(212) 535-5900, ext. 15/16

Contact Person

Alicia Driks, Coordinator.

Objectives of Library or Information Center

The Jewish Women's Resource Center aims to meet the multifaceted and ever-growing needs of the Jewish feminist community. To this end, the Center offers a large collection on all aspects of Jewish women's traditional and contemporary experience.

Access Privileges

Open to the public. Also open to social services and support groups.

Hours

Monday through Friday, 9:00–5:00.

Description of Women's Materials

Provides information about all aspects of Jewish women's experience, including Jewish "herstory," innovations in nonsexist rituals, fiction, poetry, periodicals, and dissertations by and about Jewish women. Of special interest is the large vertical file collection, which includes unpublished and obscure references. The Center has audiotapes and some works in Hebrew.

Collection by Format

Books and monographs: yes	Oral history: yes
Pamphlets: yes	Manuscripts or archives: yes

Reprints, clippings: yes   Other: dissertations and unpublished
Audiotapes: yes   works

The entire collection encompasses approximately three thousand items and is rapidly growing. Of special interest are audiotapes of the Shekhinah Conference on Women's Spirituality and Jewish Tradition; nonsexist *ketubot* (Jewish wedding contract), birth ceremonies, new prayers for women, and various support groups and programs.

Services

Telephone reference: yes   Reading room: yes
Photocopying: yes   Audiovisual facilities: yes

Publications

The Jewish Women's Resource Center has compiled a large number of bibliographies that are for sale at a nominal price. They deal with such issues as Jewish feminism, the Jewish mother, divorce, American immigrant Jewish women in the early twentieth century, women's prayers, and the like.

Additional Information

Apart from the bibliographies issued by the Library, the Center also has a number of booklets for sale, such as the *Experimental Guide to Celebrating the Birth of a Daughter, Blessing the Birth of a Daughter* by the early Jewish feminist group Ezrat Nashim, the *ketubot* packet, and the Rosh Hodesh ceremonies booklet.

96. NATIONALIST FEMINIST STUDIES INSTITUTE

Mailing Address: Feminists Concerned for Better Feminist Leadership
P.O. Box 1348 Madison Square Station
New York, New York 10159

Telephone Number

(212) 796-1467

Contact Person

Mia Albright.

Objectives of Library or Information Center

The Nationalist Feminist Studies Institute is devoted to feminist education, to inform women about the principles, strategies, and historical role of Nationalist Feminism in the context of contemporary American feminism and global feminism.

Access Privileges

Open to any interested woman by appointment.

Hours

By appointment.

Description of Women's Materials

Materials include transcripts of workshops, articles and excerpts from the basic texts, two audio cassettes, including "Feminist Personal Political Counseling," and cultural videos.

Collection by Format

Pamphlets: yes   Videotapes: yes
Audiotapes: yes   Manuscripts or archives: yes

Services

Telephone reference: yes

Publications

Bibliographies: *The Nationalist Feminist Education* (1983); *The Feminist Economy: The Social Significance of Nationalist Feminism* (1984); *Feminist Analysis Of Malist Imperialism* (1986); *Feminist Analysis of Malist Imperialism: Excerpts* (1987); and *Feminism: Freedom From Wifism* (1987).

97. NEW JERSEY DEPARTMENT OF COMMUNITY AFFAIRS

Division on Women
379 West State Street
Trenton, New Jersey 08625-0800

Telephone Number

(609) 292-8840

Contact Person

Connie Myers.

Objectives of Library or Information Center

To gather complete and accurate information about issues of concern to women in New Jersey from public and private sources.

Access Privileges

Open to the public.

Hours

Monday through Friday, 9:30–5:00.

Description of Women's Materials

Issue-oriented resource collection that includes materials on child care/welfare, domestic violence, higher education, sexual assault, employment, minority women (especially black and Hispanic), displaced homemakers and legislation. Includes census and other statistics on New Jersey women. Some information available by county.

Collection by Format

Books and monographs: 50+
Current serial titles: limited
Government documents: 50+
Pamphlets: 50+
Reprints, clippings: 100+

Videotapes and films: limited
Manuscripts or archives: limited
Other: Collection expanding under auspices of new public information officer.

Resources available to women in New Jersey listed by county.

Services

Telephone reference: yes
Photocopying: yes
Reading room: yes

Publications

Finding aids/guides: Card catalog being completed; in-house resource person.

98. THE NEW JERSEY HISTORICAL SOCIETY LIBRARY

230 Broadway
Newark, New Jersey 07104

Telephone Number

(201) 483-3939; Manuscripts, ext. 36; Reference, ext. 41

Contact Person

Sarah Collins, Library Director.

Objectives of Library or Information Center

Founded in 1845, the Library collects, preserves, interprets, displays, and provides access to printed, manuscript, and audiovisual materials that relate to New Jersey from prehistory to the present.

Access Privileges

Open to the public (noncirculating collection).

Hours

Tuesday through Saturday, 10:00–4:00; summer and holiday schedules vary.

Description of Women's Materials

There is an extensive manuscript collection (papers, scrapbooks, diaries, letters, etc.) of notable New Jersey women educators, social reformers, civic leaders, inventors, poets, writers, artists, musicians, businesswomen, and the like). The collection also includes the manuscript records of women's organizations in New Jersey, such as the Daughters of the American Revolution—Montclair Chapter, the Federal Writers Project—Women's Archives, the Female Union School Association, the National Organization of Women—Monmouth County Chapter, New Jersey Women Authors, the New Jersey Women Library Workers, the New Women Suffrage Association, the Newark Female Charitable Society, the Sabbath School for Coloured People in the Newark Academy—Female Department, the South Orange Female Organization, Trenton, New Jersey, Voluntary Associations, and the Women's Club of Orange. The archives of the New Jersey Women's Project are to be donated to the Library. The Library is also a repository for the Voices of America Homemakers Project of the New Jersey Extension Homemakers Council. The New Jersey Historical Society Museum at the same location includes materials on women artists, quilts, samplers, and so forth.

Collection by Format

Books and monographs: yes
Current serial titles: 25
Pamphlets: ca. 1,000
Reprints, clippings: extensive
Microfilm reels: dissertations

Slides: yes, in Museum collection
Manuscripts or archives: 125 Collections
Other: photographs, in Museum collection

99. NEW YORK CITY COMMISSION ON THE STATUS OF WOMEN

52 Chambers Street, Suite 207
New York, New York 10007

Telephone Number

(212) 566-3830

Contact Person

Lisa Kassel.

Access Privileges

Open to the public.

Hours

Monday through Friday, 9:00–5:00.

Description of Women's Materials

The Library's main focus is on women's issues.

Collection by Format

Books and monographs: yes　　　Government documents: yes
Pamphlets: yes　　　Reprints, clippings: yes

There are clipping files of articles dealing with women's issues from major daily newspapers and weekly magazines over the last eight years.

Services

Borrowing privileges: yes　　　Telephone reference: yes
Photocopying: yes　　　Reading room: yes

●

NEW YORK CITY COUNCIL COMMITTEE ON WOMEN

see The Council of the City of New York

100. NEW YORK CITY TECHNICAL COLLEGE

300 Jay Street
Brooklyn, New York 11201

Telephone Number

(718) 643-5240

Contact Person

Paul Sherman.

Objectives of Library or Information Center

To support the career-oriented programs offered by the College.

Access Privileges

Open to New York City Technical College students, faculty, and staff; CUNY and Academic Libraries of Brooklyn Open Access users. METRO referral card honored.

Hours

Monday through Friday, 9:00–9:00; Saturday and Sunday, 10:00–2:00.

Description of Women's Materials

The major subjects of interest included are women's rights, education and careers, abortion, contraception and pregnancy, and marriage and the family.

Collection by Format

Books and monographs: yes
Pamphlets: yes
Current serial titles: yes

Services

Telephone reference: yes
Interlibrary loan: yes
Photocopying: yes

Reading room: yes
Audiovisual facilities: yes

Publications

Bibliographies: *Women's Studies: A Guide to Multi-Media Resources.*

101. NEW YORK FEMINIST ART INSTITUTE

Women's Center for Learning
91 Franklin Street
New York, New York 10013

Telephone Number

(212) 219-9590

Contact Person

Regina Tierney.

Objectives of Library or Information Center

To be a resource for women in the arts.

Access Privileges

Open to the public and to the members. $5.00 fee for nonmembers.

Hours

Monday, Wednesday, Friday, 11:00–4:00.

Description of Women's Materials

There is a special slide library and archives of women artists (over eight hundred represented). Started in the 1970s by Lucy Lippard, it documents the work of well-known and lesser-known women all over the United States. A viewer is available.

Collection by Format

Slides: 800 artists
Manuscripts or archives: Donated collection courtesy of Lucy Lippard.

Services

Borrowing privileges: yes

Additional Information

The New York Feminist Art Institute opened in 1979 as the first art school created by women artists for women artists. The community vision was one of a vested interest in the power of women together, the importance of education, and how it can reflect and make changes in art, in society at large, and in the various communities. Today the Institute is a unique learning center that hosts a wide selection of services including space, exhibitions, dances, workshops, and performances, in addition to education.

102. THE NEW YORK GENEALOGICAL AND BIOGRAPHICAL SOCIETY LIBRARY

122 East 58 Street
New York, New York 10022

Telephone Number

(212) 755-8532

Contact Person

Betty H. Payne.

Objectives of Library or Information Center

To acquire, preserve, and make available materials on genealogy and local history.

Access Privileges

Open to the public; some parts of the collection are reserved for members; nonmember donation, $3.00, annual membership, $50.00.

Hours

Monday through Saturday, 9:30–5:00. Closed Saturdays May through September; closed August.

Description of Women's Materials

The collection includes a small number of titles on women in New York City, Indiana, Maine, Massachusetts, New York State, Rhode Island, and Pennsylvania, as well as on other topics.

Collection by Format

Books and monographs: yes
Microfilm reels: yes (for members)
Manuscripts or archives: yes (for members)

103. NEW-YORK HISTORICAL SOCIETY LIBRARY

170 Central Park West
New York, New York 10024

Telephone Number

(212) 873-3400, ext. 25, 26, 27

Contact Person

Jean Ashton, Assistant Librarian—Reference Services.

Objectives of Library or Information Center

Historical library with a particular focus on American history of the eighteenth and nineteenth centuries, particularly the history of the New York area.

Access Privileges

Open to researchers and the general public; readers must be college age or over. $2.00 for entrance to Society; $1.00 Library fee (for nonmembers).

Hours

Tuesday through Saturday, 10:00–5:00 (Monday through Friday during summer).

Description of Women's Materials

The general collections contain much original source material documenting women's activities in American history. In addition to diaries, letters, account books, etc., there is a good collection of annual reports of charitable societies, protective associations, and abolitionist organizations. There is also a particularly strong collection of nineteenth-century women's periodicals.

Collection by Format

Books and monographs: yes
Current serial titles: yes
Pamphlets: yes
Reprints, clippings: yes

Microfilm reels: yes
Manuscripts or archives: yes
Other: lithographs, photographs,
   newspapers

The manuscript collections are of more than routine interest. In addition to items mentioned above, they include apprenticeship records, wills, real estate transactions, and business papers that mention or involve women.

Services

Telephone reference: yes
Photocopying: yes

Reading room: yes
Other: mail reference service

104. NEW YORK HOSPITAL—CORNELL MEDICAL CENTER

Medical Archives
1300 York Avenue
New York, New York 10021

Telephone Number

(212) 472-5759

Contact Person

Adele A. Lerner, Archivist.

Objectives of Library or Information Center

To collect, organize, preserve, and make accessible the records of the New York Hospital, Cornell University Medical College, the School of Nursing, and affiliate institutions.

Access Privileges

Open to all qualified researchers.

Hours

Monday through Friday, 9:00–5:00; call for an appointment.

Description of Women's Materials

Containing approximately three thousand and eight hundred cubic feet of paper records and approximately ten thousand items of a pictorial nature (prints, photographs, slides, films), the Archives house a rich source of "women's material." The affiliated hospitals treat female patients and employ women as physicians, nurses, administrators, and the like. The Medical College, the Graduate School, and the School of Nursing train women. The records in the Archives often discuss so-called "proper behavior" or "proper jobs" for women. Women are also featured as philanthropists who give time and money to other women, as in the case of the New York Asylum for Lying-In Women.

Collection by Format

Books and monographs: ca. 50
Current serial titles: 2
Audiotapes: 92
Oral histories: ca. 26
Microfilm reels: 60
Reprints, clippings: ca. 500

Videotapes: 5
Archives: ca. 600 cubic feet
Slides: ca. 165
Microfiche: 3
Films: 25

Among the many important materials are the records of the Cornell University—New York Hospital School of Nursing (1877–1979), the Division of Nursing Service of New York Hospital, the Lying-In Hospital of the City of New York, the Manhattan Maternity and Dispensary, the Nursery for the Children of Poor Women, the Nursery and Child's Hospital, the New York Infant Asylum, and the New York Asylum for Lying-In Women. The papers of Drs. Connie M. Guion, Ruth M. Bakwin, Ethelyn Anderson, R.N.s Major Julia C. Stimson, Marion Doane, and others are also included, as are the records of the Navajo–Cornell Field Health Project, the Ninth General Hospital, World War II, the Society of the New York Hospital, and the New York Hospital Department of Social Service, among others. The collection also includes oral histories of R.N.s Laura Simms, Helen Berg, Virginia Dunbar, Bessie A. R. Parker, and Drs. Ruth M. Bakwin and Constance Friess, among others.

Services

Telephone reference: yes
Reading room: yes
Photocopying: yes

Audiovisual facilities: by arrangement

Publications

Finding aids/guides: *Papers of Connie M. Guion, M.D., School of Nursing papers, Division of Nursing Service Records,* etc.

Additional Information

Serves as the Archives Repository for the American Medical Women's Association in addition to the records of the New York Hospital—Cornell Medical Center.

105. NEW YORK PSYCHOANALYTIC INSTITUTE
A. A. Brill Library
247 East 82 Street
New York, New York 10028

Telephone Number

(212) 879-6900

Contact Person

David J. Ross, Librarian.

Objectives of Library or Information Center

To collect comprehensively in psychoanalysis.

Access Privileges

Open to students, practitioners, and researcher in psychoanalysis and related areas.

Hours

Monday through Thursday, 12:00–9:00; Friday, 12:00–6:00.

Description of Women's Materials

A number of women figured prominently in the history of psychoanalysis and the archival collections document their role in the Psychoanalytic Institute. Individuals' papers (e.g., Drs. Mary O'Neil Hawkins and Margaret Mahler) provide more detailed pictures of the professional and personal concerns of women in psychoanalysis, as do a number of oral history interviews with women (e.g., Drs. Marianne Kris, Dora Hartmann, Edith Jacobson, Jeanne Lampl-de Groot, Else Pappenheim, Viola Bernard, et al.).

Collection by Format

Oral history: yes
Archives: yes

Services

Telephone reference: yes   Photocopying: yes
Interlibrary loan: yes   Reading room: yes

106. THE NEW YORK PUBLIC LIBRARY

Mid-Manhattan Library
455 Fifth Avenue
New York, New York 10016

Telephone Number

(212) 340-0888, History and Social Sciences Department; 340-0873, Literature and Language Department; 340-0877, Picture Collection

Objectives of Library or Information Center

The Mid-Manhattan Library has in-depth subject collections that are geared to the needs of college undergraduates, beginning Master's candidates, and serious adult users. It forms a bridge between the general current collections of the neighborhood branches and the scholarly retrospective collections of the Research Libraries.

Access Privileges

Open to the public. METRO referral card honored.

Hours

History and Social Sciences Department, Literature and Language Department: Monday through Thursday, 9:00–9:00; Saturday, 10:00–6:00. Picture Collection: Monday, Wednesday, Friday, 10:00–6:00; Tuesday, 12:00–8:00; Thursday, 10:00–6:00; Saturday, 1:00–5:00.

Description of Women's Materials

History and Social Sciences Department: Includes a women's studies collection—history, biography, and bibliographical sources, such as *Women Studies Abstracts.* There is a small periodical collection. Both circulating and reference materials are represented.

Literature and Language Department: Includes books and recordings of fiction, drama, and poetry by women authors. Bibliographies, biographies, handbooks, and staff-compiled indexes to books and periodicals give access to critical and biographical material on these authors, as well as to "Women in Literature" and related topics.

Picture Collection: Includes specific subject files on "Women" and on "Woman Suffrage." The former category is divided by date and contains images depicting typical women's roles, famous women, and historic events unique to women as a group. The "Personalities" section of the file contains portraits of women by name. Throughout the collection, under various categories, are images of women as they appear in government, American history, industries, professions, etc.

Collection by Format

Books and monographs: yes
Current serial titles: yes
Other: pictures

Services

Borrowing privileges: yes
Telephone reference: yes
Photocopying: yes

Interlibrary loan: yes
Reading room: yes
Audiovisual facilities: yes

107. THE NEW YORK PUBLIC LIBRARY

Research Libraries
Fifth Avenue at 42 Street
New York, New York 10018

Telephone Number

(212) 930-0831

Contact Person

Elizabeth L. Diefendorf.

Access Privileges

Open to persons over eighteen years of age or in college. Use of special collections is limited to scholars and graduate students.

Hours

Vary according to division or unit.

Description of Women's Materials

The material available on women in the Research Libraries of the New York Public Library is vast and difficult to summarize. All of the divisions of the Library, from the Science and Technology Research Center, to the Map Division, to the Dance Collection, to the Schomburg Center for Research on Black Culture, have books and other items in their collections valuable for research on women. But central to the investigations of many scholars in the field are the collections of the General Research Division and the Economic and Public Affairs Division, which share overall collecting responsibility for the subject of women. For the most part the collections administered by these divisions are shelved in the closed stacks of the Central Building at Fifth Avenue and 42 Street and at the Annex at 521 West 43 Street.

Current materials on women are actively acquired. An effort has been made to buy and catalog a significant portion of the enormous number of books produced during the last two decades as a result of the women's movement and increased interest in women's lives generally. Books from trade publishers, university presses, small presses, and women's presses are all sought out. "CATNYP," the Library's online catalog which lists items added to the collection since 1972, includes 1,493 listings under the subject "feminism," 776 listings under "women and literature," and 386 listings under "abortion." Most of these listings are for recently published monographs, but periodicals devoted to these subjects are listed in CATNYP as well.

The older collections are also rich. The retrospective catalog lists many rare or unique publications, as well as most standard works by and about women that were printed in the eighteenth, nineteenth, and early twentieth centuries. Bibliography, history, anthropology, biography, autobiography, and imaginative literature by women have been collected comprehensively, as have books and periodicals on the subjects of feminism, woman suffrage, prostitution, and the social conditions of women generally. Books about women in the professions, such as S. Gregory's *Letters to Ladies in Favor of Female Physicians for Their Own Sex* (Boston, Female Medical Education Society, 1854), annual reports and other publications of women's associations, such as The Boston Female Anti-Slavery Society's *Annual Report* (1836–44), and ethnic periodicals, such as *Die Deutsche Hausfrau; Monatschrift für deutschen Frauen Amerika's,* published in Minneapolis and Milwaukee from 1907 to 1928, are all strongly represented in the collection.

The various Special Collections have extensive holdings of rare and original material, such as first editions of significant works by women, and manuscripts written by famous and obscure women from many historical periods. For instance, Manuscripts and Archives holds letters and other papers of Carrie Chapman Catt, Elizabeth Cady Stanton, and Lucy Stone; and the Berg Collection holds the largest single collection of Virginia Woolf manuscripts.

In recent years, the Library has acquired several major compilations of source material on women that commercial publishers have produced on microfilm. Foremost among these is the *History of Women* microfilm collection, which brings together monographs, pamphlets, periodicals, manuscripts, and some photographs on nearly one thousand reels of microfilm. Another example is *Herstory,* a collection of serial literature on microfilm from the International Women's History Periodical Archive.

Collection by Format

Books and monographs: yes
Current serial titles: yes
Government documents: yes
Pamphlets: yes
Reprints, clippings: some
Microfilm reels: yes
Films: in Schomburg Center and the Library of the Performing Arts

Microfiche: yes
Manuscripts or archives: yes
Audiotapes: in Schomburg Center and the Library of the Performing Arts
Videotapes: in Schomburg Center and the Library of the Performing Arts

Among the extensive manuscript and archival holdings are selected papers of Eliza Frances Burnett, Willa Cather, Carrie Chapman Catt, Lydia Maria Child, Fannia Cohn, Babette Deutsch, Dorothea Dix, Emma Goldman, Lillie Langtry, Anne O'Hare McCormick, Rose Pesotta, Genevieve Taggard, Lillian D. Wald, and others. Papers on women's organizations include the records of the Jeannette Rankin Brigade, the National American Woman Suffrage Association, the National Women's Party, the New York School of Applied Design for Women, the Stage Women's War Relief, and the Women's Peace Union, among others. For excellent description and analysis of these holdings, see: *Women's History Sources: A Guide to Archives and Manuscript Collections in the United States,* edited by Andrea Hinding, (New York: Bowker, 1979).

Services

Telephone reference: yes
Photocopying: yes
Interlibrary loan: yes
Reading room: yes

Audiovisual facilities: in Schomburg Center and the Library of the Performing Arts

Publications

Guide to the Research Collections of the New York Public Library, compiled by Sam P. Williams under the direction of William Vernon Jackson and James W. Henderson (Chicago: American Library Association, 1975).

108. THE NEW YORK PUBLIC LIBRARY

Schomburg Center for Research in Black Culture
515 Lenox Avenue
New York, New York 10037

Telephone Number

(212) 862-4000

Contact Person

Valerie Sandoval Mwalilino, Head, Acquisition Section.

Objectives of Library or Information Center

Schomburg Center's aim is to document the history and culture of peoples of African descent throughout the world. The general collection is very strong on the Afro-American population of the United States, African people on the continent, and the black population of the Caribbean, Central America, and South America.

Access Privileges

Open to researchers eighteen years old and over; identification (with name and address) required. METRO referral card honored.

Hours

Monday through Wednesday, 12:00–8:00; Thursday through Saturday, 10:00–6:00; summer hours vary.

Description of Women's Materials

The scope of women's materials generally parallels the scope of the larger collection, which emphasizes the social sciences and the humanities. Many original publications by black women writers, especially nineteenth-century Afro-American writers, can be found. There is good documentation of "black firsts," i.e., women who were the first to obtain degrees, to practice their professions, to become millionaires, and the like. The periodical collection features many publications from the United States, Africa, and the Caribbean that are specifically geared to women; there are also many organizational newsletters. Specialized finding aids are available in the Reference Department.

Collection by Format

Books and monographs: yes
Current serial titles: yes
Government documents: few

Audiotapes: yes
Videotapes: yes
Films: yes

Pamphlets: yes
Reprints, clippings: yes
Microfiche: yes
Microfilm reels: yes

Filmstrips: few
Slides: yes
Oral history: yes
Manuscripts or archives: yes

Among the many noteworthy collections are the papers of Harlem Renaissance poet Gwendolyn Bennett, actor Freddie Washington, judge Jane Bolin, physician May Chinn, Cuban actor Eusebia Cosme, librarian Sadie P. Delany, and entertainers Mabel Mercer and Ada "Bricktop" Smith. The oral history videotape collections include interviews with Lillian Roberts and Katherine Dunham, among others.

Services

Telephone reference: yes
Photocopying: yes
Interlibrary loan: yes

Reading room: yes
Audiovisual facilities: yes

Publications

Bibliographies: see issues of *Schomburg Center Journal* (quarterly)
Finding aids/guides: *Kaiser Index to Black Resources* (not yet published)

Additional Information

Schomburg Center also regularly sponsors educational and cultural programs as well as quarterly exhibits in the first floor gallery and reading rooms. Travelling exhibits are available for loan.

109. THE NEW YORK PUBLIC LIBRARY AT LINCOLN CENTER

General Library and Museum of the Performing Arts
111 Amsterdam Avenue
New York, New York 10023

Telephone Number

(212) 870-1630; Dance Information Desk, 870-1627; Drama Information Desk, 870-1627; Music Information Desk, 870-1625; Record Information Desk, 870-1629

Objectives of Library or Information Center

To collect and provide access to resources in the performing arts—dance, drama, and music.

Access Privileges

Open to the public. A New York Public Library card is necessary to borrow materials.

Hours

Monday, Tuesday, Thursday, 10:00–8:00; Wednesday, Friday, 12:00–6:00; Saturday, 10:00–6:00; summer hours are shorter. Hours may vary from year to year. Call 870-1630 for hours.

Description of Women's Materials

The Library attempts to acquire all important materials on women in the performing arts. The Dance Collection does not have a separate collection of books or files on women in dance, but given the important role that women have played in dance, particularly in the twentieth century, the collection contains a large number of books and clippings by and about female dancers and choreographers. The Drama Collection contains books and vertical file material on women in cinema, television, and theatre. This information focuses on women as creative artists, as well as the portrayal of women in these disciplines. The Music Collection contains books on women in music (including bibliographies and discographies), musical scores of music by women composers, and clipping files of newspaper and periodical articles about women composers and performers. The Record Collection includes dance and dramatic materials by women, as well as records whose subject is women in society, such as feminist recordings.

Collection by Format

Books and monographs: yes
Current serial titles: yes

Audiotapes: yes
Videotapes: yes

Pamphlets: yes   Other: scores
Reprints, clippings: yes

Services

Borrowing privileges: with New York   Photocopying: yes
Public Library card   Interlibrary loan: yes
Telephone reference: yes   Reading room: yes

Publications

Periodicals received: yes
Bibliographies: Discographies on *Women in Music.*

110. THE NEW YORK PUBLIC LIBRARY AT LINCOLN CENTER

Performing Arts Research Center
The Billy Rose Theatre Collection
111 Amsterdam Avenue
New York, New York 10023

Telephone Number

(212) 870-1636

Contact Person

Dorothy L. Swerdlove, Curator.

Objectives of Library or Information Center

To provide information on individuals, organizations, and productions in the performing arts (stage, film radio, television, vaudeville, circus, magic, puppetry, industrial shows, amusement parks, etc.).

Access Privileges

Open to adult readers (eighteen years or older) or college students.

Hours

Monday, Thursday, 10:00–7:45; Tuesday, Wednesday, Friday, 12:00–5:45; Saturday, 10:00–5:45. (Summer hours, from Memorial Day through Labor Day, are somewhat shorter—no evening hours.)

Description of Women's Materials

Information on women in the performing arts. Archival collections include the papers of Margaret Anglin, Ilka Chase, Katharine Cornell, Cheryl Crawford, Glenda Farrell, Nancy Hamilton, Helen Hayes, Gertrude Lawrence, Lenka Peterson, Sophie Tucker, Dora Weissman, and Blanche Yurka.

Collection by Format

Books and monographs: yes
Current serial titles: yes
Slides: yes
Pamphlets: yes
Government documents: yes
Microfilm reels: yes

Archives: yes
Microfiche: yes
Videotapes: yes
Costume and scenery designs: yes
Reprints, clippings: yes

Collection of radio scripts by Elaine Carrington; costume designs by Bonnie Cashin; costume/scenery designs by Aline Bernstein.

Services

Interlibrary loan: limited
Reading room: yes
Photocopying: limited

Telephone reference: limited
Audiovisual facilities: yes
Borrowing privileges: for exhibitions only

111. NEW YORK STATE DEPARTMENT OF LABOR

Research Library—New York City
Two World Trade Center, Room 6826
New York, New York 10047

Telephone Number

(212) 488-6295; 488-6296

Contact Person

Gloria Weinrich, Ashley Hibbard.

Objectives of Library or Information Center

The Library serves the research and information needs of the New York State Department of Labor.

Access Privileges

Open to the public for information not available in the public or college libraries.

Hours

Monday through Friday, 9:00–4:30.

Description of Women's Materials

Subjects covered include women workers, discrimination (employment, education), comparable worth, nontraditional occupations, and the economic problems of women. There is a special collection of the Women's Trade Union League materials.

Collection by Format

Books and monographs: yes
Government documents: yes
Current serial titles: yes

Pamphlets: yes
Reprints, clippings: yes
Microfiche: yes

Services

Borrowing privileges: yes
Interlibrary loan: yes

Photocopying: yes
Reading room: yes

112. NEW YORK STATE PSYCHIATRIC INSTITUTE LIBRARY

722 West 168 Street
New York, New York 10032

Telephone Number

(212) 960-5672

Contact Person

David Lane.

Objectives of Library or Information Center

To support the research carried out by the Institute.

Access Privileges

Open to outside users for in-house use only. (No circulating materials.)

Hours

Monday through Thursday, 9:00–8:00; Friday, 9:00–5:00; Saturday, 10:00–5:00.

Description of Women's Materials

The collection includes books on sex roles and on the psychiatric and psychological aspects of women.

Collection by Format

Books and monographs: 50
Current serial titles: 5

Services

Photocopying: yes
Interlibrary loan: yes
Reading room: yes

Publications

Periodicals received: yes

113. NEW YORK UNIVERSITY

Elmer Holmes Bobst Library
70 Washington Square South
New York, New York 10012

Telephone Number

(212) 598-3601, Information Desk

Contact Person

Polly Thistlethwaite, 598-2048.

Objectives of Library or Information Center

To serve the information and research needs of the students and faculty of New York University and the larger research community.

Access Privileges

Open to students, faculty, and staff of New York University; also open to students and faculty of the New School, Parsons, and Cooper Union, as well as to members of the Research Libraries Group. METRO referral card honored. Fees for reading privileges for members of Friends of Bobst Library and Alumni Association.

Hours

Monday through Thursday, 8:30 A.M.–11:00 P.M.; Friday, 8:30–7:00; Saturday, 10:00–6:00; Sunday, 2:00–10:00. Hours vary during holidays, summer, and examinations.

Description of Women's Materials

The sociology, anthropology, psychology, business and economics, literature, history, and performing arts collections contain materials on women's studies. There is an international, pan-ethnic focus on sociocultural and economic issues.

Collection by Format

Books and monographs: yes
Current serial titles: yes
Government documents: yes
Microfilm reels: yes

Microfiche: yes
Videotapes: yes
Manuscripts or archives: yes

Services

Telephone reference: yes
Interlibrary loan: yes
Reading room: yes

114. NEW YORK UNIVERSITY

Elmer Holmes Bobst Library
Fales Library
70 Washington Square South
New York, New York 10012

Telephone Number

(212) 988-2596

Contact Person

Frank Walker, Head of Special Collections.

Objectives of Library or Information Center

The Fales Library houses New York University's Special Collections, of which the Fales Collection of English and American Fiction is the largest.

Access Privileges

Open to qualified researchers. METRO referral card honored.

Hours

Monday through Thursday, 2:00–5:00; other times by appointment.

Description of Women's Materials

The Elizabeth Robins Papers is an extensive archive containing the letters, diaries, notebooks, manuscripts, scrapbooks, photographs, legal and financial records, and other files of printed material of the American actor, novelist, playwright, and suffragist. Robins's long life (1862–1952) saw her involvement in theatrical, literary, and social movements over several decades, and her archive represents a major resource for feminist studies.

Collection by Format

Books and monographs: 4 feet
Manuscripts or archives: 100 feet
Reprints, clippings: 5 feet

Services

Reading room: yes

Publications

Finding aids/guides: *The Elizabeth Robins Papers,* by Janet Evander and Marion Casey.

115. NEW YORK UNIVERSITY

Tamiment Library
Robert Wagner Labor Archives
70 Washington Square South
New York, New York 10012

Telephone Number

(212) 598-7708/7754

Contact Person

Dorothy Swanson, Head Librarian.

Objectives of Library or Information Center

The Tamiment Library is a unique center for scholarly research pertaining to labor and radical movements.

Access Privileges

Open to any researcher having a need to use unique research materials. METRO referral card honored.

Hours

Monday, Thursday, 10:00–9:00; Tuesday, Wednesday, Friday, 10:00–6:00; Saturday, 10:00–5:00.

Description of Women's Materials

The manuscript collections include papers of Emma Goldman, Helen Tufts Bailie, Lena Morrow Lewis, Rose Schneiderman, Rose Pastor Stokes, and Mrs. Philip Taft, among others, as well as papers on the Department Stores Strikes and Organizing in the 1930s, and the United Hat, Cap, and Millinery Workers International Union.

Collection by Format

Books and monographs: yes
Current serial titles: yes
Pamphlets: yes
Microfilm reels: yes

Audiotapes: yes
Oral history: yes
Manuscripts or archives: yes

Services

Photocopying: yes
Interlibrary loan: yes

116. NEW YORK WOMEN STRIKE FOR PEACE

799 Broadway
New York, New York 10003

Telephone Number

(212) 254-1925

Contact Person

Celia Fink.

Objectives of Library or Information Center

New York Women Strike for Peace is a women's peace organization that generates activities for a reversal in the arms race, and for the promotion of disarmament and peace.

Access Privileges

Open to the public. Membership fee $25.00 per year; low-income fee $15.00 per year.

Description of Women's Materials

There are newsletters, leaflets, and descriptive pamphlets relating to the issues of "End the Arms Race—Not the Human Race."

Collection by Format

Pamphlets: yes
Reprints, clippings: yes

117. NEW YORK WOMEN'S BAR ASSOCIATION COMMITTEE ON BATTERED WOMEN

15 East 40 Street
Room 904-5
New York, New York 10016

Telephone Number

(212) 889-7873

Contact Person

Mae Link.

Hours

By arrangement.

Description of Women's Materials

The collection includes materials on violence against women and children, with particular emphasis on legal rights and legal issues.

Collection by Format

Books and monographs: 30
Government documents: 10
Pamphlets: 10

Reprints, clippings: hundreds
Audiotapes: 3
Videotapes: 3

There are documents relating to legislative reform on rape, battering, and child sexual abuse from 1979 to the present. There are also materials from six Annual Conferences on the Legal Rights of Battered Women in New York State. The archives and materials are on services and issues in New York City from 1976 through the present.

118. NEWARK PUBLIC LIBRARY

5 Washington Street
Newark, New Jersey 07101-0630

Telephone Number

(201) 733-7784

Contact Person

Humanities, Reference, or Social Science Division.

Objectives of Library or Information Center

To meet the educational, informational, cultural, aesthetic, and recreational needs of the people of Newark. The Newark Public Library is one of New Jersey's three research libraries.

Access Privileges

Open to the public; borrowing privileges limited to cardholders. METRO referral card honored. $10.00 per year fee for library card.

Hours

Monday, Wednesday, Thursday, 9:00–9:00; Tuesday, Friday, 9:00–5:30; Saturday, 9:00–5:00; Sunday, 1:00–5:00.

Description of Women's Materials

The emphasis is on African-American studies (both the social sciences and the humanities), with a study-level collection on women's materials. The women's studies materials are integrated into the Library's holdings.

Collection by Format

Books and monographs: yes
Current serial titles: yes
Pamphlets: yes
Reprints, clippings: yes
Filmstrips: yes

Microfilm reels: *Women's History Library—First Series*
Government documents: regional depository

Services

Borrowing privileges: yes
Telephone reference: yes

Interlibrary loan: yes
Reading room: yes

119. 92ND STREET YM—YWHA ARCHIVES

1395 Lexington Avenue
New York, New York 10128

Telephone Number

(212) 427-6000, ext. 215

Contact Person

Steven W. Siegel.

Objectives of Library or Information Center

The 92nd Street Y Archives preserve the historical record of the current organization (a Jewish community center) and of several defunct women's organizations that merged with the 92nd Street Y.

Access Privileges

Open to the public.

Hours

Monday through Friday, by appointment.

Description of Women's Materials

The women's materials consist primarily of the archival records of two defunct women's organizations: The Young Women's Hebrew Association (1902–1945) and the Clara de Hirsch Home for Working Girls (1897–1962).

Collection by Format

Manuscripts and archives: 10 cubic feet

Services

Photocopying: yes
Reading room: yes

Publications

Finding aids/guides: *Guide to the Records of the Clara de Hirsch Home for Working Girls; Guide to the Records of the Young Women's Hebrew Association.*

Additional Information

The bulk of the records preserved in the 92nd Street Y Archives deals with the activities of the Young Men's Hebrew Association (1874–1945) and the Young Men's and Young Women's Hebrew Association (1945–present). Materials relating to women's activities and programs, and women who have spoken, performed, etc. at the Y, may be found in the overall archives. However, these latter materials are not physically segregated as "women's materials."

120. O.D.N. PRODUCTIONS, INC.

74 Varick Street, Suite 304
New York, New York 10013

Telephone Number

(212) 431-8923

Contact Person

Monica Wolfson, Marketing/Distribution Director.

Objectives of Library or Information Center

O.D.N., a nonprofit educational media company, produces and distributes films, videotapes, and curricular materials to a variety of organizations for use as a resource or curriculum base.

Access Privileges

Open to individuals, counseling/mental health/medical clinics, church groups, government agencies, schools/universities, health/human services, educational and volunteer organizations, and the like. Please write for an appointment. Fees for purchase, rentals, and previews of films and videos.

Hours

Monday through Friday, 9:00–5:00.

Description of Women's Materials

Educational "trigger" films, training films, accompanying curriculum materials and public awareness media on subjects that range from AIDS prevention to date rape, domestic violence, child sexual abuse prevention, teen pregnancy prevention, and parent education. These films and videotapes are currently in use in schools and training programs in the United States and overseas.

Collection by Format

Pamphlets: yes
Reprints, clippings: yes
Videotapes: yes
Films: yes

Other: Most films and videos are accompanied by print curriculum/study guides.

One of O.D.N.'s recent video projects was to produce a thirty-second public service announcement for the New York Coalition Against Domestic Violence, which was broadcast on national network television in 1984. This announcement (or the poster version) is available to shelters and clinics for purchase.

Services

Borrowing privileges: yes
Telephone reference: yes
Interlibrary loan: yes (fee)

Other: films, videos, and public service announcement available for purchase

Additional Information

O.D.N. is managed by a staff of six women with backgrounds in education and media technology.

121. OYSTERPONDS HISTORICAL SOCIETY

Village Lane
Orient, New York 11957

Telephone Number

(516) 323-2480

Contact Person

Jean Martin, Director; Donald Boerum, Head Librarian.

Access Privileges

Open to the Society's members; open to the public by appointment ($2.00 fee for nonmembers).

Description of Women's Materials

The Oysterponds Historical Society has a fairly extensive collection of women's materials. There are women's magazines from the late nineteenth century, a photograph collection that documents women's fashion from 1860 to 1920 (two thousand photographs), diaries of women from eastern Long Island, a manuscript copy of excerpts from Mrs. E. P. Brown's diary aboard a whaling vessel, ca. 1848, and a costume collection of women's garments (including bonnets, jewelry, fans, and the like). There is an exhibit of four women (the Tuttles) who were little people. They worked as seamstresses during the mid-nineteenth century, in Orient, and the exhibit includes their clothing, shoes, and other possessions.

Collection by Format

Manuscripts or archives: yes

Services

Telephone reference: limited
Photocopying: certain types
Reading room: yes

Publications

Finding aids/guides: In process of cataloging. A retrieval system is under development.

Additional Information

The Society owns the home of Amanda Brown, who was a nineteenth-century schoolteacher, and her one-room classroom. It also owns Webb House, the oldest house on Long Island to have been built as an inn, and Village House, a boarding house that was managed by a woman (Mrs. Vail).

122. PARSONS SCHOOL OF DESIGN

Adam and Sophie Gimbel Design Library
2 West 13 Street
New York, New York 10012

Telephone Number

(212) 741-8915

Contact Person

Sharon Chickanzeff.

Objectives of Library or Information Center

To support all facets of the Parsons curriculum (fine arts, industrial design, environmental design, illustration, communication arts, crafts, fashion history and design, and graphic design.

Access Privileges

Open to Parsons students, consortium (New York University/New School/ Cooper Union) users, and the interested public. METRO referral card honored. Fees for photocopying.

Hours

Monday through Thursday, 9:00–9:00; Friday, 9:00–6:00, Saturday, 10:00– 6:00; summers, Monday through Friday, 9:00–6:00.

Description of Women's Materials

Parsons does not have a separate collection of women's materials, but it makes a concerted effort to collect all monographs on women artists, architects, designers, and the like, including a substantial resource of international exhibition catalogs. Areas of historical concern include the representation of women in art and advertising, and the history of costume. Special collections include the fashion sketchbooks of Claire McCardell.

Collection by Format

Books and monographs: yes   Current serial titles: yes
Slides: yes   Other: sketchbooks

Services

Telephone reference: limited
Photocopying: yes
Interlibrary loan: Research Libraries Group members only

Publications

Periodicals received: yes

123. THE PIERPONT MORGAN LIBRARY

29 East 36 Street
New York, New York 10016

Telephone Number

(212) 685-0008, ext. 376

Contact Person

Inge Dupont, Supervisor of the Reading Room.

Objectives of Library or Information Center

The Pierpont Morgan Library is a museum and research library that has as its focus art, history, and literature.

Access Privileges

The reading room is open to accredited scholars, graduate research students, curators and librarians, and book dealers and collectors owning comparable material, upon written application and by appointment.

Hours

Monday through Friday, 9:30–4:45; closed last two weeks in August.

Description of Women's Materials

There is a small collection of reference books on women in art and literature.

Collection by Format

Books and monographs: yes
Pamphlets: yes
Reprints, clippings: yes

Microfilm reels: yes
Slides: yes
Manuscripts or archives: yes

The collection of authors' original autographed manuscripts contains some letters and manuscripts written by women.

Services

Telephone reference: yes
Reading room: yes
Photocopying: of some reference materials

Publications

Finding aids/guides: Sample subject entries in catalog include women, women in literature and art, and women as printers.

124. PLANNED PARENTHOOD FEDERATION OF AMERICA, INC.

Katharine Dexter McCormick Library
810 Seventh Avenue
New York, New York 10019

Telephone Number

(212) 603-4637

Contact Person

Gloria A. Roberts, Head Librarian.

Objectives of Library or Information Center

To provide information on family planning, population, reproductive rights issues, sexuality education and human sexuality to the general public, as well as to the staff.

Access Privileges

Open to the public by appointment. METRO referral card honored.

Hours

Monday through Friday, 9:15–4:30.

Description of Women's Materials

The McCormick Library has special collections on Margaret Sanger and women involved in the birth control movement, women's health, maternal and child care, contraception, sex roles, sexuality, reproductive rights, the women's movement, and the status of women.

Collection by Format

Books and monographs: yes   Pamphlets: yes
Current serial titles: yes   Reprints, clippings: yes

The McCormick Library has a collection of four thousand volumes, over fifty thousand articles and clippings, and one hundred and seventy-five journals on population, family planning, and sexuality education. The material is cataloged and indexed in accordance with a special classification scheme. A vertical file collection arranged by this numerical scheme provides instant in-depth coverage of a topic. Card catalogs for authors and subjects, both arranged alphabetically, complete the major focus of access to the collection.

Services

Telephone reference: yes

Photocopying: yes

Interlibrary loan: yes

Reading room: yes

Publications

Bibliographies: *Current Literature in Family Planning* (monthly classified review of the books and journal articles); there are numerous bibliographies and database searches on adolescent sexuality, birth planning decisions, issues of the 1980s, men and sexuality, the politics of sexuality education, religion and family life education, school sexuality education, sexuality and the disabled, and sexually transmitted diseases. Other publications include *A Family Planning Library Manual* (1982) and *A Small Library in Family Planning* (1980; 1987 edition in progress).

PLANNED PARENTHOOD FEDERATION OF AMERICA, INC.

125. PLANNED PARENTHOOD OF NEW YORK CITY

Abraham Stone Memorial Library
380 Second Avenue
New York, New York 10010

Telephone Number

(212) 777-2002, ext. 3158

Contact Person

Jeanne Swinton.

Objectives of Library or Information Center

To document the social issues concerning family planning, adolescents, women's reproductive health care, abortion, and the training of nonphysician health personnel (nurse midwives and practitioners) for research and educational purposes.

Access Privileges

Open to the public by appointment.

Collection by Format

Books and monographs: yes   Pamphlets: yes
Current serial titles: yes   Reprints, clippings: yes

The Library includes the Christopher Tietze Collection on pregnancy termination worldwide and its relationship to primary health care.

Services

Telephone reference: yes
Photocopying: yes
Reading room: yes

126. POETRY SOCIETY OF AMERICA

The Van Voorhis Library
Fifteen Gramercy Park
New York, New York 10003

Telephone Number

(212) 254-9628

Contact Person

Kristine Chalifoux.

Objectives of Library or Information Center

To maintain a vital and growing repository of books by and about American poets.

Access Privileges

Open to the public by appointment.

Hours

Monday through Friday, 10:00–4:00.

Description of Women's Materials

The Van Voorhis Library has resources on American poetry, biography, and criticism. There are some holdings on foreign poets. The holdings of major American women poets from 1900 to the present are substantial.

Collection by Format

Books and monographs: 8,000
Audiotapes: yes (few)

Manuscripts or archives: yes
Other: chapbooks

Services

Borrowing privileges: yes
Telephone reference: yes

Photocopying: yes
Reading room: yes

127. PORT WASHINGTON PUBLIC LIBRARY

245 Main Street
Port Washington, New York 11050

Telephone Number

(516) 883-4400, ext. 103; Media Services, ext. 140

Contact Person

Virginia Parker.

Objectives of Library or Information Center

To provide public library service.

Access Privileges

Open to the public (for reference use only).

Hours

Monday through Friday, 9:00–9:00; Saturday, 9:00–5:00; Sunday (October through March), 1:00–5:00.

Description of Women's Materials

The Library has oral history materials that include interviews with Afro-American women in Port Washington for some six generations (interviews conducted mainly between 1981 and 1984; one conducted in 1964). There are (both audio and video) tapes of Sardinian women describing their lives in Port Washington from the 1880s to the 1980s (interviews conducted in 1983). There are also tapes of women who worked on the great estates of Long Island as cooks, parlormaids, laundresses, and nurses from the 1890s to the 1940s (interviews conducted from 1985 to the present). Other tapes focus on local women who are involved in educational, cultural, and social institutions. The Library's archives include the Hewitt collection of correspondence, financial records, and a Civil War diary of key women members of the family. There are also nineteenth-century school books and photo albums for the period from the 1780s to the 1930s. The Library has a collection of videotapes of women photographers that document a series of gallery talks. This series includes tapes on Berenice Abbott, Diane Arbus, Laura Gilpin, Barbara Kasten, Lisette Model, Joan Myers, and Starr Ockenga. There are also a number of tapes by women videomakers, such as Doris Chase and Deanna Kamiel.

Collection by Format

Videotapes: 3
Oral history audiotapes: 23
Oral history transcripts: 21

Manuscripts or archives: 5 linear feet
Photographs: ca. 100

128. PRINCETON UNIVERSITY

Firestone Library
Princeton, New Jersey 08544

Telephone Number

(609) 452-3180

Contact Person

Women's Studies Selector or Supervisor of Holden Collection.

Objectives of Library or Information Center

To support the teaching and research of Princeton University.

Access Privileges

Open to Princeton University community; outside users should contact Access Office; fee may be charged, call (609) 452-5737.

Hours

Access: Monday through Friday, 8:00–5:00; Saturday, 9:00–1:00, 2:00–5:00. Firestone: Monday through Friday, 8:00 A.M.–11:45 P.M.; Saturday, Sunday, 9:00 A.M.–11:45 P.M.

Description of Women's Materials

A general women's studies collection is dispersed in the Firestone stacks and in the branch libraries. The Miriam Y. Holden Collection on the History of Women is a special collection on the history, condition, and achievements of women, collected by a noted private collector. It consists of some four to five thousand items and includes a noncirculating collection of books and serials that is housed in a separate room in Firestone, as well as rare books and manuscripts. There is a Women's Studies Pamphlet File, a collection of pamphlets and clippings from the late 1960s to the mid 1970s. It includes pamphlets purchased from the Women's History Research Center in Berkeley. There is an index by subject, author, and title. The Pamphlet File is housed in the Reference Room at Firestone.

Collection by Format

Books and monographs: yes
Current serial titles: 90
Government documents: yes
Pamphlets: 15 drawers
Reprints, clippings: yes

Audiotapes: yes
Microfilm reels: yes
Microfiche: yes
Manuscripts or archives: yes

Services

Borrowing privileges: for a fee
Telephone reference: yes
Photocopying: yes

Interlibrary loan: yes
Reading room: yes
Audiovisual facilities: yes

129. QUEENS COLLEGE LIBRARY

65-30 Kissena Boulevard
Flushing, New York 11367

Telephone Number

(718) 520-7255

Contact Person

Anna Brady.

Objectives of Library or Information Center

To serve the students, faculty, and staff of Queens College and the broader community.

Access Privileges

Open to the public for on-site access to materials. METRO referral card honored.

Hours

Monday through Thursday, 9:00–9:00; Friday, 9:00–5:00; Saturday and Sunday, 12:00–5:00.

Description of Women's Materials

The general undergraduate library collection includes materials relevant to women's studies (socialization and sex roles; history; employment; specific cultural, ethnic, and racial groups; education; etc.) but there is not any special strength in this area.

Collection by Format

Books and monographs: yes
Government documents: yes
Current serial titles: yes

Pamphlets: yes
Microfilm reels: yes

Services

Borrowing privileges: available to college community only
Interlibrary loan: available to college community only

Photocopying: yes
Reading room: yes

Publications

Bibliographies: *Women's Studies: A Guide to Resources.*

130. QUEENSBOROUGH COMMUNITY COLLEGE LIBRARY

56 Avenue and Springfield Boulevard
Bayside, New York 11364

Telephone Number

(718) 631-6241

Contact Person

Carol Sanger.

Objectives of Library or Information Center

To support the curriculum and the instructional program of the College.

Access Privileges

Open to CUNY students, staff, and faculty. METRO referral card honored.

Hours

Monday through Thursday, 8:30 A.M.–9:00 P.M.; Friday, 8:30–5:00; Saturday, 10:00–5:00; call for summer hours.

Description of Women's Materials

The collection is a basic one. It includes books and monographs on all major subjects of interest to women's studies, as well as pamphlets that offer career information.

Collection by Format

Books and monographs: 500   Government documents: 100
Current serial titles: 4   Pamphlets: 100

Services

Borrowing privileges: yes   Interlibrary loan: yes
Telephone reference: yes   Audiovisual facilities: yes
Photocopying: yes

Publications

Bibliographies: *Woman's History Bibliography.*

ROBERT J. KIBBEE LIBRARY

see Kingsborough Community College

●

ROBERT WAGNER LABOR ARCHIVES

see New York University

131. ROCKEFELLER ARCHIVE CENTER

Pocantico Hills
North Tarrytown, New York 10607

Telephone Number

(914) 631-4505

Contact Person

J. William Hess, Associate Director.

Objectives of Library or Information Center

To preserve and make available to scholars the records of The Rockefeller University, The Rockefeller Foundation, Rockefeller Brothers Fund, members of the Rockefeller family, and other individuals and organizations associated with their endeavors.

Access Privileges

Open to qualified scholars.

Hours

Monday through Friday, 9:00–5:00.

Description of Women's Materials

The records of The Rockefeller Foundation, Laura Spelman Rockefeller Memorial, Bureau of Social Hygiene, General Education Board, Population Council, and the Rockefeller family include files relating to social problems, education, child study, parent education, birth control, maternal health, nursing, vocational status, and suffrage. A few women were officers of these organizations and women involved with various organizations were correspondents.

Collection by Format

Manuscripts or archives: yes

The Bureau of Social Hygiene (1911–1940) was especially concerned with social problems relating to women. The Laura Spelman Rockefeller Memorial conducted a major program in child study and parent education.

Services

Photocopying: for visiting scholars
Reading room: yes

Publications

Finding aids/guides: *Archives and Manuscripts in the Rockefeller Archive Center* (1984); *A Survey of Manuscript Sources for the History of Nursing in the Rockfeller Archive Center* (1985).

132. RUTGERS, THE STATE UNIVERSITY OF NEW JERSEY

Center of Alcohol Studies
Smithers Hall, Busch Campus
Piscataway, New Jersey 08854

Telephone Number

(201) 932-4442

Contact Person

Penny Page, Librarian.

Objectives of Library or Information Center

To collect and disseminate research information on all aspects of alcohol and its use and related problems.

Access Privileges

Open to the public. Photocopies are $.10 per page; borrower's card for nonRutgers patrons is $50.00 per year.

Description of Women's Materials

The Center contains books and reprints on women's use of alcohol; medical, psychological, and social consequences of women's alcohol use; sex-role, self-esteem, and women's alcohol use; and treatment and prevention of alcohol problems among women.

Collection by Format

Books and monographs: yes
Pamphlets: yes
Government documents: yes

Reprints, clippings: yes
Microfilm reels: yes

Services

Borrowing privileges: yes
Photocopying: yes
Telephone reference: yes

Interlibrary loan: yes
Reading room: yes

Publications

Bibliographies: *Women and Alcohol.*

133. RUTGERS, THE STATE UNIVERSITY OF NEW JERSEY

Eagleton Institute of Politics
Center for the American Woman and Politics
New Brunswick, New Jersey 08901

Telephone Number

(201) 828-2210

Contact Person

Kathy Kleeman, Research Associate.

Objectives of Library or Information Center

The Center aims to develop and disseminate information about United States women's political participation and to encourage women's involvement in public life.

Access Privileges

Open to students and faculty at Rutgers University and to other interested individuals.

Hours

Monday through Friday, 9:00–4:00.

Description of Women's Materials

The Center for the American Woman and Politics maintains a reference (noncirculating) collection of materials about women's political participation. It focuses on women and/in politics. It also contains materials on the contemporary women's rights movement.

Collection by Format

Books and monographs: ca. 600
Current serial titles: ca. 45

Government documents: yes
Reprints, clippings: yes

There is an extensive collection of published, unpublished, and working papers; newspaper clippings, magazine and journal articles housed in a vertical file system and organized by subject. The papers and reports are cataloged by subject and author, with headings based on the women's studies thesaurus developed by the National Council for Research on Women. CAWP maintains a computerized database with listings for more than eighteen thousand elected women at local, state, and federal levels all over the country. A documentary film, "Not One of the Boys" (1984), examines the progress women are making in public office after a decade of increasing involvement in the political process.

in public office after a decade of increasing involvement in the political process.

Publications

Periodicals received: yes

The Center publishes *News & Notes: About Women Public Officials,* a newsletter issued three times a year that reports on activities of women in public life around the nation and lists events, contact people, and resource ideas, as well as fact sheets on women in elective and appointive office. Among the many publications issued by the Center are those devoted to women in legislative leadership, women candidates and their campaigns, public leadership education programs for women, leaders of organizations of women public officials, women in municipal management, women's organizations in the public service, lobbying, and the like.

134. RUTGERS, THE STATE UNIVERSITY OF NEW JERSEY

Institute of Jazz Studies
135 Bradley Hall
Newark, New Jersey 07102

Telephone Number

(201) 648-5595; 648-5801

Contact Person

Vincent Pelote, Librarian.

Objectives of Library or Information Center

The Institute is an archive of jazz and jazz-related materials. The archive is engaged in collection development, preservation, cataloging, and the organization of materials and a wide variety of public services.

Access Privileges

Open to scholars and researchers with an interest in jazz. METRO referral card honored. Fees for taping and photocopying.

Hours

Monday through Friday, 9:30–5:30, except for University holidays.

Description of Women's Materials

There are resources on women in jazz (instrumentalists and vocalists), with background materials on Afro-Americans, race relations, and numerous sociological issues.

Collection by Format

Books and monographs: 25
Oral history: 5
Manuscripts or archives: yes

Sound recordings: extensive
Reprints, clippings: clipping files

The collection of jazz phonograph records is extensive. The archival collection includes materials on Mary Lou Williams.

Services

Telephone reference: yes
Photocopying: yes
Interlibrary loan: yes

Reading room: yes
Audiovisual facilities: yes (listening, taping facilities)

Additional Information

The Institute of Jazz Studies, founded in 1952, is a major research archive of jazz sound recordings, books on jazz, jazz periodicals from throughout the world, clippings, photographs, music manuscripts, films, African instruments, and memorabilia. It is a valuable resource for researchers studying jazz music, ethnomusicology, social studies, Afro-American history, social documentation, and related areas. Jazz scholars from all sections of the United States and many foreign countries find the Institute's resources essential to their research, for the updating and for compilation of jazz and jazz-related discographies and bibliographies, and for the documentation and verification of data prior to the publication of journal articles and monographs.

135. RUTGERS, THE STATE UNIVERSITY OF NEW JERSEY

Mabel Smith Douglass Library/Archibald Stevens Alexander Library
New Brunswick, New Jersey 08903

Telephone Number

(201) 932-9407

Contact Person

Francoise S. Puniello, Women's Studies Bibliographer, Douglass Library.

Objectives of Library or Information Center

To serve the informational needs of women's studies research at the University and, secondarily, of the community at large.

Access Privileges

Open to all. METRO referral card honored.

Hours

Variable. Douglass Library: Monday through Thursday, 8:00 A.M.–11:00 P.M.; Friday, 9:00–5:00; Saturday, 9:00–5:00; Sunday, 12:00–11:00.

Description of Women's Materials

Materials on history, literature, political science, sociology, anthropology, gender roles, women in science, women in the arts (two libraries combined). Douglass owns some papers of Elizabeth Cady Stanton and a women's file (a pamphlet collection).

Collection by Format

Two libraries combined:
Books and monographs: 9,500
Current serial titles: 94
Government documents: ca. 1,000
Microfilm reels: see below
Pamphlets: 260 folders (Douglass)
Audiotapes: 89 (Douglass)

Videotapes: 29 (Douglass)
Films: 100
Slides: 8 sets (Douglass)
Manuscripts or archives: 125 collections of papers and records

The Alexander Library microfilm collection includes the National Women's Party papers, *History of Women* (216 reels), June Addams papers, and Women, Industry and Trade Unionism. The Douglass Library microfilm collection includes *Herstory* and *Women in Law.*

Services

Telephone reference: yes
Photocopying: yes
Interlibrary loan: yes

Reading room: yes
Audiovisual facilities: yes

Publications

Bibliographies: At Douglass, *Women: Guide to Resources in the Douglass Library.*

Additional Information

There is no designated women's studies library among the eighteen Rutgers libraries. Since the Mabel Smith Douglass Library, which serves Douglass College, has made a concerted effort since 1970 to collect women's studies materials, its collection, as well as that of Alexander Library (the social science and humanities research library), are included in the survey. In terms of book count, it would be difficult to enumerate all the books that might have an impact on the study of women's lives, so only the books in the Library of Congress classification HQ are given.

136. ST. FRANCIS COLLEGE

McGarry Library
180 Remsen Street
Brooklyn, New York 11201

Telephone Number

(718) 522-2300, ext. 205

Contact Person

Joan Torrone.

Objectives of Library or Information Center

To serve students, faculty, staff, and alumni of St. Francis College.

Access Privileges

Open to the Academic Libraries of Brooklyn. METRO referral card honored.

Hours

Monday through Thursday, 8:30–8:15; Friday, 8:30–5:00; Saturday, 9:00–2:00.

Description of Women's Materials

St. Francis had long been a men's school, and the collection on women's materials is still minimal but is approaching a "decent" size.

Collection by Format

Books and monographs: yes
Manuscripts or archives: yes

There is some archival material on women in Brooklyn.

Services

Telephone reference: yes   Interlibrary loan: yes
Photocopying: yes   Reading room: yes

Publications

Accession lists: yes
Periodicals received: yes

ST. MARK'S LIBRARY

see General Theological Seminary

137. ST. MARK'S WOMEN'S HEALTH COLLECTIVE, INC.

9 Second Avenue
New York, New York 10003

Telephone Number

(212) 228-7482, 228-7483

Contact Person

Ulle Koiv, Coordinator.

Objectives of Library or Information Center

To provide women, especially lesbians, with information on women's health issues from a range of health care disciplines from traditional Western to alternative and Eastern care.

Access Privileges

Open to women, especially lesbians, from any geographic area, of any age.

Hours

During the evening hours of the Health Center; check message tape.

Description of Women's Materials

The collection focuses on physical and mental health from a lesbian perspective. Included are directories of health and community resources, material on how to choose a health care provider, materials on donor insemination, research on lesbian health issues, general medical texts and references, nutritional information, etc.

Collection by Format

Books and monographs: 75   Pamphlets: 24
Government documents: 12   Videotapes: 1

Donor insemination information/instructions for the process for lesbians, including birthing information, available with or without the associated program at the Health Center. Videotape on breast cancer for lesbians also available.

Services

Reading room: yes
Other: one-to-one instruction or education

Additional Information

This is not a formal collection. It is a resource consisting of three bookshelves and a videotape. The Collective's clients find it an interesting and valuable aid in their participation in maintaining their health and well being.

138. ST. VINCENT'S HOSPITAL

Rape Crisis Program
153 West 11 Street
New York, New York 10011

Telephone Number

(212) 790-8068; 790-8069

Contact Person

Wendy Levine.

Access Privileges

Open to all.

Hours

Monday through Friday, 9:00–5:00, by appointment.

Description of Women's Materials

Resources on rape: legal, medical, and political (including feminist theory, racism, homophobia); rape trauma syndrome; incest; "special" populations—the disabled, the elderly, etc.; battering; male rape; the offender; date rape; marital rape (some).

Collection by Format

Books: yes
Government documents: yes
Pamphlets: yes

Reprints, clippings: yes
Videotapes and films: referrals

The library has reprints of many articles written by renowned people in the field.

Services

Photocopying: yes

Publications

Bibliographies: Books only.

139. SALVATION ARMY ARCHIVES AND RESEARCH CENTER

145 West 15 Street
New York, New York 10011

Telephone Number

(212) 620-4392

Contact Person

Thomas Wilsted, Archivist/Administrator.

Objectives of Library or Information Center

To collect, preserve, and make available the official records and private papers created by the Salvation Army and by individual Salvationists.

Access Privileges

Open to Salvationists and members of the public (specific collections may have restricted access). Fees for photocopying only.

Hours

Monday through Friday, 8:30–4:00; closed major holidays.

Description of Women's Materials

The Archives reflect a variety of activities that involve women. These include records of rescue homes for prostitutes, homes for unwed mothers, and homes for orphans and children. The collection contains a variety of records on women Salvation Army officers who were given equal status as ordained ministers at the time the Salvation Army was founded in 1878. The collection reflects a wide variety of social services and religious issues facing women in the United States. Approximately one-third of the collection deals with women.

Collection by Format

Books and monographs: yes
Microfilm reels: yes
Slides: yes
Microfiche: yes
Current serial titles: yes
Reprints, clippings: yes

Audiotapes: yes
Videotapes: yes
Films: yes
Pamphlets: yes
Manuscripts: yes
Archives: yes

Records on significant women include those devoted to General Evangeline Booth, Catherine Booth, Emma Booth-Tucker, Maud Ballington Booth, Emma Jane Brown, Cecil Brown, Blanche B. Cox, Agnes H. McKernan, Hilda Plummer, Florence A. Turkington, Jane Elizabeth Wreiden, and Helen Purviance.

Services

Telephone reference: yes
Reading room: yes
Photocopying: yes

Audiovisual facilities: yes
Interlibrary loan: microfilm only

Publications

General newsletter *(Historical News-Views)*
Bibliographies: in process
Finding aids/guides: Unpublished guides to archival collection.

SANFORD V. LENZ LIBRARY

see Cornell University/New York State School of Industrial and Labor Relations

140. SARAH LAWRENCE COLLEGE

Esther Raushenbush Library
Bronxville, New York 10708

Telephone Number

(914) 337-0700, ext. 474

Contact Person

Rose Anne Burstein, Library Director.

Objectives of Library or Information Center

To serve the undergraduate population and a graduate program in women's history (the first in the nation).

Access Privileges

Open to the public for on-site use. METRO referral card honored. As of January 1987, 60 percent of collection is on OCLC (the Online Computer Library Center).

Hours

Monday through Thursday, 8:30 A.M.–10:00 P.M.; Friday and Saturday, 11:00–7:00; Sunday, 11:00–10:00; call for summer and vacation hours.

Description of Women's Materials

The Library has strong holdings on all aspects of women's studies, with a special focus on history, education, the social sciences, alternative politics, women artists, and women poets. There is a large collection of women's autobiographies, a comprehensive collection of United States Women's Bureau *Bulletins,* the *Report on Conditions of Women and Child Wage Earners in the United States* (1910–1913, partial holdings), selected papers of the International Women's League for Peace and Freedom, and selected papers of Mercedes Randall on the League.

Collection by Format

Books and monographs: 10,000+
Current serial titles: 80+
Government documents: yes (United States government repository)
Pamphlets: yes
Manuscripts or archives: yes

Microfilm reels: 100+
Microfiche: yes
Audiotapes: yes
Videotapes: yes
Slides: yes
Oral history: yes

The collection of nineteenth-century periodicals and newspapers is of special note. The Library has *Herstory* on microfilm, some of the papers of Genevieve Taggard and Helen Merrell Lynd, and oral histories of many of the women instrumental in founding Sarah Lawrence College, such as Esther Raushenbush, Lois Barclay Murphy, and Ermine "Pebble" Stone.

Services

Telephone reference: yes   Interlibrary loan: yes
Photocopying: yes   Reading room: yes

Publications

Periodicals received: *Periodicals of Special Interest to Women* and *Women's Studies: Current Periodical Subscriptions.*
Bibliographies: *Bibliography on the History of Women in the Progressive Era,* by Judith Papachristou (1986); *Bibliography in the History of European Women,* by Joan Kelly, revised by K. Casey, P. Charles, and B. Engel; *Women and the American Experience,* by Gerda Lerner (1975).
Finding aids/guides: *Women's Studies: Reference Sources;* finding aid list to the archival holdings of Helen Merrell Lynd.
    The Library also has the Master's theses of the Women's History Program, with circulating copies available for most theses.

●

SCHOMBURG CENTER FOR RESEARCH IN BLACK CULTURE

see The New York Public Library

141. SETON HALL UNIVERSITY

McLaughlin Library
400 South Orange Avenue
South Orange, New Jersey 07079

Telephone Number

(201) 761-9431, Circulation Desk

Contact Person

Barbara Geller, Archivist, (201) 761-9476.

Objectives of Library or Information Center

To serve the University community.

Access Privileges

Open to University community and County of Essex Cooperating Libraries System (CECLS).

Hours

Please call Circulation Desk for current information.

Description of Women's Materials

The Library has a basic collection of women's materials. Of note is the Seton-Jevons Collection—family papers, diaries, and correspondence. Archives also contain a history of the Nursing School.

Collection by Format

Books and monographs: yes
Current serial titles: yes

Government documents: yes
Manuscripts or archives: yes

Services

Borrowing privileges: to University
   community and CECLS members
Photocopying: yes

Reading room: yes
Interlibrary loan: yes, through OCLC
Other: Telefacsimile (201) 761-9432

142. SEX INFORMATION AND EDUCATION COUNCIL OF THE UNITED STATES (SIECUS)

Mary S. Calderone Library
32 Washington Place, Room 52
New York University
New York, New York 10003

Telephone Number

(212) 673-3850

Contact Person

Leigh Hallingby, Manager.

Objectives of Library or Information Center

To provide information on all aspects of human sexuality and sex education.

Access Privileges

Open to the public.

Hours

New York University academic year: Monday through Thursday, 1:30–8:00; Friday, Saturday, 9:00–1:00; summer: call for hours.

Description of Women's Materials

The Library has materials on female sexuality, lesbianism, sex roles, female sex dysfunction, sexual abuse of children, rape, and the like.

Collection by Format

Books and monographs: yes   Pamphlets: yes
Current serial titles: yes   Reprints, clippings: yes

There are periodical articles, sex education curricula, audiovisual catalogs, and other materials.

Services

Telephone reference: yes   Reading room: yes
Photocopying: yes   Other: mail reference

Publications

Bibliographies: *Human Sexuality: A Bibliography for Everyone* (1987). Single copies available for $1.00 with a stamped, self-addressed envelope. Other SIECUS bibliographies cover resources for professionals in areas such as sex and family life education curricula, child sexual abuse education and prevention, AIDS, human sexuality audiovisuals, sexuality and disability, and religious publications on sexuality and sex education.

●

SIECUS

see Sex Information and Education Council of the United States

143. SOCIETY OF WOMEN ENGINEERS

345 East 47 Street
New York, New York 10017

Telephone Number

(212) 705-7855

Contact Person

B. J. Harrod.

Objectives of Library or Information Center

To inform young women, their parents, counselors, and the general public of the qualifications and achievements of women engineers.

Access Privileges

Open to all members, student members, and those interested in women in engineering.

Hours

Monday through Friday, 9:00–5:00.

Description of Women's Materials

The Society does not have a library. It does, however, have materials on women in engineering, such as its magazine, *U.S. Woman Engineer,* its biennial survey of its membership, *A Profile of the Woman Engineer,* and other guidance materials. Some of these materials are for sale.

Collection by Format

Pamphlets: yes
Audiotapes: yes
Videotapes: yes

Films: yes
Filmstrips: yes
Slides: yes

SOPHIA F. PALMER LIBRARY

see American Journal of Nursing Co.

•

144. STATE UNIVERSITY OF NEW YORK AT ALBANY

Center for Women in Government
Draper Hall, Room 302
1400 Washington Avenue
Albany, New York 12222

Telephone Number

(518) 442-3900

Contact Person

Audrey Seidman, Public Information Director.

Objectives of Library or Information Center

The Center for Women in Government was founded in 1978 to remove barriers to the employment and promotion of women in the public sector. Since then, the Center has gained national recognition for innovation and leadership in its work to achieve equal employment opportunity for women. The Center's program includes research, training, technical assistance, public education, and the implementation of responsible civil service reform.

Description of Women's Materials

The Center produces publications for sale on pay equity, affirmative action, career ladders, sexual harassment, women in management, and the like.

Collection by Format

Books and monographs: yes
Pamphlets: yes

145. STATE UNIVERSITY OF NEW YORK AT OLD WESTBURY LIBRARY

Storehill Road, Box 229
Old Westbury, New York 11568

Telephone Number

(516) 876-3151

Contact Person

Wagih Shenouda, Head of Reference.

Objectives of Library or Information Center

To serve the curricular needs of students and faculty.

Access Privileges

Open to all interested persons; any individual with valid SUNY identification card may borrow books. METRO referral card honored.

Hours

Monday through Thursday, 8:45 A.M.–10:00 P.M.; Friday, 8:45–6:00; Saturday, 12:00–5:00; Sunday, 2:00–10:00. Contact Reference Department for holiday and intersession hours.

Description of Women's Materials

The collection covers women's history, literature, and culture in the United States and around the world (with emphasis on current imprints). This includes narratives and materials on women's experiences, issues, and problems. The Women's History Research Center Microfilm Library is available. The periodicals received on women's studies cover a large variety of subject areas.

Collection by Format

Books and monographs: 2,554
Current serial titles: 9
Government documents: yes

Films: 2
Microfilm reels: 144
Videotapes: 15

Of special interest: *Herstory I* (microfilm) 1956–June 1974; *Herstory II* (microfilm) October 1971–June 1974; *Herstory III* (microfilm) July 1973–June 1974; *Women & Health/Mental Health* (microfilm) Section 1–7; *Women & Law* (microfilm) Section 1–6.

Services

Borrowing privileges: yes (SUNY ID)
Telephone reference: yes
Photocopying: yes

Interlibrary loan: yes
Reading room: yes
Audiovisual facilities: yes

Publications

Bibliographies: *Recent Acquisitions,* issued twice a year, has a section on Women's Studies.

146. STATE UNIVERSITY OF NEW YORK AT PURCHASE LIBRARY

Purchase, New York 10577

Telephone Number

(914) 253-5096

Contact Person

Paula Hane, Humanities Reference Librarian.

Access Privileges

Open to the public for on-site use. METRO referral card honored.

Hours

Monday through Thursday, 8:30 A.M.–11:45 P.M.; Friday, 8:30–4:45; Saturday, 12:00–4:45; Sunday, 1:00–11:45. Academic holidays and vacations, Monday through Friday, 8:30–4:45. Summer, as announced.

Description of Women's Materials

The collecting emphasis is on the history of women, particularly women and work and the labor movement, radical feminists, diaries, feminist literary criticism, women in literature, women in the performing and visual arts, and gender and sex roles.

Collection by Format

Books and monographs: yes
Current serial titles: 30

Government documents: yes
Microfilm reels: yes

Services

Telephone reference: yes
Photocopying: yes
Interlibrary loan: yes

Reading room: yes
Audiovisual facilities: yes

Publications

Periodicals received: yes

147. STATE UNIVERSITY OF NEW YORK AT STONY BROOK

Melville Library
Stony Brook, New York 11733

Telephone Number

(516) 632-7110

Contact Person

Barbara B. Brand.

Objectives of Library or Information Center

To support university-level instruction and research.

Access Privileges

Open to the public.

Hours

Monday through Thursday, 8:30 A.M.–12:00 midnight; Friday, 8:30 A.M.–10:00 P.M.; Saturday, 10:00–6:00; Sunday, 2:00–12:00.

Description of Women's Materials

The collection includes material on women's socialization and sex roles, psychology of women, history of women, literature and criticism of women (in the major European languages as well as English); legal, economic, and social status of women, feminist theory, anthropology of women, and women and politics.

Collection by Format

Books and monographs: 20,000+
Government documents: 2,000+
Current serial titles: 35
Microfilm reels: 300

Microfiche: 2,200
Videotapes: 20
Manuscripts or archives: yes

Microform collections: American Women's Diaries (New England); Cornell University Collection of Women's Rights Pamphlets; Gerritsen Collection of Women's History, 1543–1945 (selected periodicals in English and French); *Herstory;* United States Department of Labor, Women's Bureau *Bulletins* and *Special Bulletins.*

   Archives: Papers and records of local chapters of NOW and the League of Women Voters; Papers of Helen Hull Jacobs 1908– relating to the WAVES; books by Marie Charlotte Stopes, suffragist and sex educator; suffrage and sex pamphlets collection; Papers of Eugenie Soderberg, 1903–1973, Swedish journalist; Papers and records of the Parkway Nursery School, Levittown, New York, 1957–76; women's history ephemera.

Services

Telephone reference: yes
Interlibrary loan: yes
Reading room: yes

Audiovisual facilities: yes
Photocopying: yes

148. STATEN ISLAND HISTORICAL SOCIETY LIBRARY

441 Clarke Avenue
Staten Island, New York 10306

Telephone Number

(718) 351-1617, ext. 209

Contact Person

Stephen Barto, Charles Sachs.

Objectives of Library or Information Center

To collect information on the history of Staten Island and its people, as well as on American history.

Access Privileges

Open to the public by appointment.

Hours

Monday through Friday, 9:00–5:00.

Description of Women's Materials

The Library has material on women's roles in the community, clothing, life in a nineteenth-century village and community, education, children, and cultural information.

Collection by Format

Books and monographs: yes	Slides: yes
Reprints, clippings: yes	Oral history: yes
Films: yes	Manuscripts or archives: yes

The costume collection is also of note.

Services

Telephone reference: yes
Photocopying: yes
Reading room: yes

149. SUFFOLK COUNTY COMMUNITY COLLEGE LIBRARY

Ammerman Campus
533 College Road
Selden, New York 11787

Telephone Number

(516) 451-4182

Contact Person

Frances M. Kelly.

Objectives of Library or Information Center

To serve the needs of the Community College.

Access Privileges

Open to all Suffolk County residents.

Hours

During academic semester: Monday through Thursday, 8:00 a.m.–10:00 p.m.; Friday, 8:00–5:00; Saturday, 8:30–1:30. At other times: Monday through Friday, 9:00–4:00.

Description of Women's Materials

There is a general women's studies collection relevant to community colleges with women's studies programs.

Collection by Format

Books and monographs: yes
Current serial titles: yes
Government documents: yes
Pamphlets: yes
Microfilm reels: yes
Microfiche: yes

Audiotapes: yes
Videotapes: yes
Films: yes
Filmstrips: yes
Slides: yes

Services

Interlibrary loan: yes
Audiovisual facilities: yes

150. SUFFOLK MARINE MUSEUM

West Sayville, New York 11796

Telephone Number

(516) 567-1733

Contact Person

Ruth Dougherty.

Objectives of Library or Information Center

The Suffolk Marine Museum is a marine library, concentrating on Great South Bay, Fire Island, shipwrecks, and boat-building in the south shore area.

Access Privileges

Open to researchers by appointment.

Hours

Tuesday through Saturday, 10:00–3:00.

Description of Women's Materials

There is little material about women other than minimal information on some early women lighthouse keepers.

Collection by Format

Books and monographs: yes
Pamphlets: yes
Reprints, clippings: yes

Services

Telephone reference: yes
Photocopying: yes

SWIRBUL LIBRARY

see Adelphi University

●

TAMIMENT LIBRARY

see New York University

151. TEACHERS COLLEGE, COLUMBIA UNIVERSITY

Milbank Memorial Library
525 West 120 Street
New York, New York 10027

Telephone Number

(212) 678-3494

Contact Person

Donna Barkman, Assistant Director and Chief for Collection Services.

Objectives of Library or Information Center

Milbank Memorial Library collects and maintains materials that reflect the historic commitment of Teachers College to advanced study in the education, psychology, and health service professions in their local, national, and international dimensions.

Access Privileges

Open to Columbia University students, faculty, staff, and constituents; on-site use card available through Library administration office for others. METRO referral card honored. Fee of $50.00 per month for borrowing privileges.

Hours

Main collection: Monday through Thursday, 10:00–10:00; Friday through Saturday, 10:00–6:00; Sunday, 1:00–9:00. Special collections: Monday, Tuesday, Thursday, Friday, 10:00–6:00; Wednesday, 10:00–9:00; special schedule for holiday and intersession periods.

Description of Women's Materials

Milbank Memorial Library has one of the largest and richest collections of materials in the world on the educating, psychological, and health service professions. Print, nonprint, and computer-generated materials are collected. The Library collects comprehensively in American elementary and secondary education, psychology, child development, educational administration, history and philosophy of education, higher and adult education, health and nursing education, nutrition, home and family life, and international and comparative education.

The special collections of Milbank Memorial Library provide extensive and unique resources in the fields of education, nursing, and psychology. Rare books, photographs, archives, and manuscript collections relate to varied aspects of women's history including the development of the nursing and teaching professions; the role of Progressive reformers in the areas of public health and early childhood education; and the formation of manual arts and domestic science as areas of study.

Among the major manuscript and archival collections are the New York City Board of Education archives which include nineteenth- and twentieth-century records, and an extensive photography collection documenting the emergence and professionalization of teaching; the Nursing Education Department archives which include the papers of distinguished nursing leaders, such as Mary Adelaide Nutting and Isabel Stewart, documenting women's role in the health sciences and the development of nursing as a profession; and the records of the National Kindergarten Association, a leading agency of the kindergarten movement in the United States.

Book collections include extensive holdings of American and foreign elementary and secondary textbooks; a resource for the study of the socialization of girls; rare books in education that include pedagogical literature and household instruction manuals of the eighteenth and nineteenth centuries; and an extensive collection of cookbooks.

Collection by Format

Books and monographs: yes
Current serial titles: yes
Manuscripts or archives: yes

Services

Telephone reference: yes
Photocopying: yes
Interlibrary loan: yes
Reading room: yes
Audiovisual facilities: yes

On-line searching: yes
Borrowing privileges: with payment of $50.00 per month fee for users not affiliated with Columbia University

Publications

Accession lists: monthly subject listing; annual *Bibliographic Guide to Education,* by G. K. Hall.
Periodicals received: annual keyword publication

152. UNION THEOLOGICAL SEMINARY

The Burke Library
3041 Broadway (at Reinhold Niebuhr Place)
New York, New York 10027

Telephone Number

(212) 662-7100, ext. 276

Contact Person

Seth Kasten, Reference Librarian.

Objectives of Library or Information Center

Primarily, to serve the library needs of the students, faculty, and staff of Union Theological Seminary and affiliate institutions; secondarily, to assist qualified nonaffiliated readers as resources permit.

Access Privileges

Open to qualified researchers who have exhausted their local library resources. METRO referral card honored. Fees: free reading for a few days' use; then, $10.00 per week plus refundable deposit of $100.00. Borrowing not normally available.

Hours

Monday through Friday, 9:00–5:00, during academic semester; call for current schedule (662-7100, ext. 273).

Description of Women's Materials

The Library has materials on women and religion; women in ministry; and women in the Bible.

Collection by Format

Books and monographs: over 2,000
Pamphlets: yes
Current serial titles: yes

Microfilm reels: yes
Manuscripts or archives: yes
Microfiche: yes

Some archival items relating to Emilie Briggs (author and teacher), Mrs. William Adams Brown (Young Women's Christian Association), Fidelia Coon (typescripts of letters to Titus Coon, 1830–48), Sophia Lyon Fahs (early twentieth-century religious educator), and Mathilda Thurston (founder and president of Gin Ling Women's College in China).

Services

Telephone reference: yes
Interlibrary loan: for fee

Photocopying: yes
Reading room: yes

153. UNITED STATES DEPARTMENT OF LABOR, WOMEN'S BUREAU

Room 601
201 Varick Street
New York, New York 10014

Telephone Number

(212) 944-3444

Contact Person

Miriam Williams.

Objectives of Library or Information Center

To provide economic and legal data and other information about women, women workers, women's issues, and the Bureau's target groups (minority women, mature and re-entry women, displaced homemakers, young women, women offenders and ex-offenders, low-income women, rural women, and women business owners).

Access Privileges

Open to the public.

Hours

Monday through Friday, 8:30–5:00.

Description of Women's Materials

The holdings of the Women's Bureau are on the history of the Women's Bureau, women workers, careers and job options, child care, standards and legislation affecting women, conference and program models, and the like.

Collection by Format

Books and monographs: yes   Pamphlets: yes
Government documents: yes   Videotapes: yes

Services

Borrowing privileges: videotape (2 weeks)
Telephone reference: when feasible
Photocopying: limited

Publications

Finding aids/guides: *Publications of the Women's Bureau.*

Additional Information

The Women's Bureau is the only federal agency devoted exclusively to the concerns of women in the labor force. Its major objective is to improve the economic status of all women through participating in the development of policy and programs that have an impact on women's employment and their employability, and through working with target groups of women with special employment-related needs to develop programs to meet those needs. The Women's Bureau is particularly concerned about certain groups of women who have not been able to enter the economic mainstream because they experience difficulties in obtaining training or jobs, or in advancing in their present employment. Their difficulties may be related to sex, age, and race discrimination or to social, economic, or geographical conditions.

Additional information is available from the Superintendent of Documents, U.S. Government Printing Office, Washington, D.C. 20402.

154. UNITED STATES MILITARY ACADEMY

West Point, New York 10996

Telephone Number

(914) 938-2954

Contact Person

Egon Weiss.

Objectives of Library or Information Center

To support the curriculum for the cadets and faculty of the United States Military Academy. The focus of the collection other than that of a general undergraduate institution is on the military history of the United States, especially as it relates to United States Military Academy graduates.

Access Privileges

Open to scholars who contact the Head Librarian by mail with their specific requests.

Hours

Monday through Friday, 8:00–4:30.

Description of Women's Materials

Women in the military: to include "Project Athena" (reports on the integration of women cadets), vertical files on women in the military, oral histories gathered by Dr. Steve Grove, in-house-generated statistics on women at West Point.

Collection by Format

Government documents: 12
Pamphlets: 15–20
Oral history: 6 years of interviews with graduating women (most not yet transcribed)
Other: 1 box (6 inches) of vertical file information

Services

Interlibrary loan: yes
Reading room: yes
Photocopying: machine available (depending upon nature of document to be copied)

155. VASSAR COLLEGE LIBRARY

Poughkeepsie, New York 12601

Telephone Number

(914) 452-7000, ext. 2125

Contact Person

Bernice K. Lacks.

Objectives of Library or Information Center

To support the educational program of Vassar College, an undergraduate college with a program in liberal arts and pure sciences.

Access Privileges

Open to members of the Vassar community and visiting scholars. Fees: $10.00 per year for those eligible.

Hours

During academic semester: Monday through Thursday, 8:30 A.M.–12:00 midnight; Friday, 8:30 A.M.–10:00 P.M.; Saturday, 9:00 A.M.–10:00 P.M.; Sunday, 10:00 A.M.–12:00 midnight. At other times: Monday through Friday, 8:30–5:00.

Description of Women's Materials

There is an extensive monographic collection with large holdings in women's history in the United States, women's diaries and autobiographies, women and economics, women and employment, women's literature, and feminist theory.

Collection by Format

Books and monographs: extensive
Current serial titles: yes
Government documents: extensive
Microfilm reels and microfiche: 45
  collections

Manuscripts or archives: 80 collections
Other: music scores and sound recordings

The Library also contains *Herstory* and the Gerritsen Collection of Women's History periodicals.

Services

Interlibrary loan: yes
Reading room: yes
Audiovisual facilities: yes

Photocopying: yes
Other: Course-related instruction

Publications

Bibliographies: many titles
Finding aids/guides: many titles

●

156. WESTCHESTER COUNTY HISTORICAL SOCIETY

**75 Grasslands Road
Valhalla, New York 10595**

Telephone Number

(914) 592-4338

Contact Person

Elizabeth G. Fuller, Librarian.

Hours

Variable; please call.

Description of Women's Materials

There are only a few materials on women—photographs, clippings, and other
biographical information chiefly on prominent Westchester women.

157. WHITE PLAINS HIGH SCHOOL LIBRARY

550 North Street
White Plains, New York

Telephone Number

(914) 997-2179

Contact Person

Merabeth Moore.

Objectives of Library or Information Center

To provide a standard secondary school collection primarily for curriculum support.

Access Privileges

Open to users on-site only. METRO referral card honored.

Hours

Monday through Friday, 8:30–2:00.

Description of Women's Materials

The Library is in the process of building a literature collection for a secondary-level women's studies course.

Collection by Format

Books and monographs: 100

Publications

Bibliographies: in process of being developed.

158. WOMEN AGAINST PORNOGRAPHY

358 West 47 Street
New York, New York 10036

Telephone Number

(212) 307-5055

Contact Person

Evelina Kane.

Objectives of Library or Information Center

To educate the public on pornography's impact on the safety and status of women.

Access Privileges

Open to the public by appointment.

Hours

Monday through Friday, 10:00–5:00.

Description of Women's Materials

The collection contains extensive material on pornography, both research and theoretical in nature. Examples: The influence of pornography on advertising, social science studies on pornography and aggression, the role of pornography in sexual abuse and battery, misogyny in rock video, dial-a-porn, pornography as racism, pornography and disability, pornography and the law (civil rights perspectives).

Collection by Format

Books and monographs: yes
Government documents: yes
Pamphlets: yes
Reprints, clippings: yes

Slides: yes
Oral history: yes
Manuscripts or archives: yes

Women Against Pornography has a slide show that is presented with a speaker for $200.00. The presentations range from "Roles in Rock" to the "Adult Slide Show." Victims' testimony material is extensive.

Services

Photocopying: yes
Reading room: yes
Audiovisual facilities: yes

Publications

Bibliographies: *General Research Bibliography; Bibliography on Child Sexual Abuse; Bibliography on Social Science Studies on Pornography.*

Women Against Pornography publishes a *NewsReport* for its members at $15.00 per year. There are also information packets for sale.

Additional Information

Women Against Pornography is both an educational and an activist organization. It has lectured throughout the country on pornography and its effects on women. It is especially known for its slide presentations and for its feminist-guided tour of the pornography district.

159. WOMEN ARTISTS NEWS/MIDMARCH ARTS

300 Riverside Avenue
New York, New York 10025

Telephone Number

(212) 666-6990

Contact Person

Cynthia Navaretta, Executive Editor.

Objectives of Library or Information Center

To serve as a center of information and an archive on women in the visual arts.

Access Privileges

Open to the public by appointment.

Hours

By special arrangement.

Description of Women's Materials

The collection is devoted to women and the visual arts—painting, sculpture, graphics, and photography; schools and colonies; influential administrative women (museum and gallery directors). There is some material on other arts—dance, music, film.

Collection by Format

Books and monographs: yes   Slides: yes
Current serial titles: yes   Manuscripts or archives: yes
Reprints, clippings: yes   Photographs: yes

The collection is a comprehensive one on women in the visual arts. There are folders for more than two thousand individual artists, with photographs, slides, and material such as resumes, catalogs, exhibition announcements, and reviews.

Services

Telephone reference: yes
Photocopying: yes

Publications

Midmarch issues a bi-monthly publication of current materials, *Women Artists News*. It also publishes a *Guide to Women's Arts Organizations* (updated every two to three years), *Women Artists of the World, Voices of Women,* and *Pilgrims and Pioneers: New England Women in the Arts,* the first in a series on regional women artists.

Additional Information

Midmarch Associates is a not-for-profit, multiservice arts organization that was founded in 1972 to implement projects of art in public places, coordinate conferences, and conduct art feasibility studies. Its periodical, *Women Artists News,* contains a comprehensive listing of women's exhibition and arts activities, including slide calls, exhibitions, panels and conferences, and news stories and regular columns covering the arts. In 1980 it administered and coordinated the International Festival of Women Artists, held in Copenhagen in conjunction with the United Nations World Conference on Women. In 1985 Midmarch provided multi-arts exhibitions for the mid-decade United Nations Conference in Nairobi, documenting the conference with a special issue of *Women Artists News.* It also serves as a sponsoring agency for unincorporated arts groups, providing guidance, information, and resources, and assuming fiscal responsibility and accountability. Midmarch maintains an Educational Internship Program in Arts Publishing for high school and college students, training them in many aspects of publishing and arts administration and offering school credit for work-site experience.

WOMEN IN SCIENCE COLLECTION

see Brookhaven National Laboratory

●

160. WOMEN IN THE ARTS FOUNDATION, INC.

325 Spring Street, Room 200
New York, New York 10013

Telephone Number

(212) 691-0988

Contact Person

Marisa Walters.

Objectives of Library or Information Center

To provide information on the history of the women's art movement and discrimination against women artists.

Access Privileges

Open by appointment only.

Collection by Format

Books and monographs: yes   Pamphlets: yes
Reprints, clippings: yes   Slides: yes

161. WOMEN MAKE MOVIES

225 Lafayette Street
New York, New York 10012

Telephone Number

(212) 925-0606

Contact Person

Debra Zimmerman.

Objectives of Library or Information Center

Women Make Movies is a feminist film distribution organization, making films and videotapes produced by and about women available to the general public.

Access Privileges

Telephone for film rental to schedule previews in the study center. Varying fees.

Description of Women's Materials

The available films include those that focus on women and work, women's health, menopause, battered women, women's literature, sex roles and machismo, women in the Third World, Latin American women, and feminist film theory. There is a special collection of films on women in Latin America.

Collection by Format

Videotapes: 50
Films: 55

Services

Telephone reference: yes

162. WOMEN'S ACTION ALLIANCE

370 Lexington Avenue, Suite 603
New York, New York 10017

Telephone Number

(212) 532-8330

Contact Person

Sylvia Kramer, Executive Director.

Objectives of Library or Information Center

The Alliance's purpose is to develop educational programs and services that assist women and women's organizations to accomplish their goals.

Access Privileges

Open to the public by appointment. Suggested contribution $3.00.

Hours

Monday through Friday, 9:30–5:30.

Description of Women's Materials

The Alliance's library includes materials on a wide range of issues of concern to women and women's groups. It is especially strong in the area of education. There are profiles of more than five hundred national and professional women's organizations. There is also a comprehensive collection of information on local, multi-service women's centers, as well as materials on program planning, organizational development, and fundraising.

Collection by Format

Books and monographs: yes   Pamphlets: yes
Current serial titles: yes   Reprints, clippings: yes

Services

Photocopying: yes
Reading room: yes

Publications

The Alliance issues *Equal Play,* a biannual national journal on nonsexist education for teachers, parents, specialists, and others concerned with issues of sex equity in education. Among the other publications of the Alliance are *Struggling through Hard Times* (1984), *Women Helping Women: A State-by-*

State Directory of Services (1981), *How to Organize a Multi-Service Women's Center* (1976), *Getting Your Share: An Introduction to Fundraising* (1976), *The Nuts and Bolts of NTO: Non-Traditional Occupations*, by Jo Shucat-Sanders (1981), and *Time for a Change: A Women's Guide to Non-Traditional Occupations*, by Constance Drake Cauley (1981). There is also a *Resource Bibliography on Women's History for Elementary and Junior High School Teachers*, by Ellise Gonzalez.

Additional Information

The Women's Action Alliance, Inc., founded in 1971, is a national organization committed to full equality for women. Its Information Services provides information on women's issues and programs to individuals and organizations by telephone, mail, in person, and through its publications. It also provides people in need with telephone referral to local service agencies. Its Sex Equity in Education Program (SEEP), formerly the Non-Sexist Child Development Project, provides assistance to educators, parents, and caregivers of Women's Action Alliance children from birth through school age in creating learning environments that are free of bias due to sex, as well as race, national origin, or disability. SEEP conducts research and development projects, creates and distributes educational materials, publishes a biannual journal, provides training and technical assistance, and participates in scholarly and practitioner conferences.

●

WOMEN'S BUREAU

see United States Department of Labor

163. WOMEN'S FUNDING COALITION

817 Broadway, Sixth Floor
New York, New York 10003

Telephone Number

(212) 677-1001

Contact Person

Karen Zelermyer.

Objectives of Library or Information Center

To provide information on funding for women's organizations and services.

Access Privileges

Open to the public by appointment.

Hours

Monday through Friday, 10:00–6:00.

Description of Women's Materials

The Coalition does not have a library. It does, however, have news clippings on issues of interest to women. Its focus is on women and philanthropy, patterns of giving to women, on United Way and women, on the need for funding women's issues, and the like.

Collection by Format

Government documents: yes
Pamphlets: yes

Reprints, clippings: yes
Slides: yes

Services

Telephone reference: yes

164. WOMEN'S INTERNATIONAL LEAGUE FOR PEACE AND FREEDOM

New York Metropolitan Branch
201 West 13 Street
New York, New York 10011

Telephone Number

(212) 242-4610

Contact Person

Anne Florant.

Objectives of Library or Information Center

To collect material dealing with the work of the Women's International League for Peace and Freedom.

Access Privileges

The materials are located in the Swarthmore College Library.

Description of Women's Materials

The Women's International League materials focus on the League's work on peace and freedom.

165. WOMEN'S INTERNATIONAL RESOURCE EXCHANGE (WIRE)

2700 Broadway
New York, New York 10025

Telephone Number

(212) 666-4622

Contact Person

Sybil Wong.

Objectives of Library or Information Center

To provide low-cost written materials (pamphlets, articles, etc.) on women in the Third World.

Access Privileges

Materials available by mail only; catalogs available on request.

Description of Women's Materials

The collection includes materials on the various aspects of women's studies, with emphasis on Latin and Central America, South East Asia, the Middle East, and Africa. There are some Spanish-language materials. The collection on Nicaraguan women is of note.

Collection by Format

Books and monographs: yes
Pamphlets: yes
Reprints, clippings: yes

166. WOMEN'S NATIONAL BOOK ASSOCIATION

Archives
Columbia University, Butler Library
New York, New York 10027

Telephone Number

(212) 280-5153

Objectives of Library or Information Center

To record the history of the Women's National Book Association, founded in 1917 by a group made up mostly of women booksellers. The WNBA's interests now include all aspects of book publishing endeavors. The organization serves as a vital reference to the history of both women and men in publishing.

Access Privileges

Open to qualified scholars.

Hours

Monday through Friday, 9:00–4:45. Please call Archivist before visiting.

Description of Women's Materials

The Archives contain the correspondence and reports of WNBA–NYC and of the WNBA national organization, as well as the national newsletter, *The Bookworm,* and the Chapter newsletters.

Collection by Format

Books and monographs: yes
Pamphlets: yes

Reprints, clippings: yes
Manuscripts or archives: yes

The collection includes the WNBA (formerly Constance Lindsay Skinner) Award records—awards given to outstanding women in publishing.

Services

Photocopying: yes
Reading room: yes

167. THE WOMEN'S PROJECT AND PRODUCTIONS, INC.

American Place Theatre
111 West 46 Street
New York, New York 10036

Telephone Number

(212) 246-3730

Contact Person

Suzanne Bennett.

Objectives of Library or Information Center

To provide scholars and theatre professionals access to unpublished plays by women for research and production.

Access Privileges

Open to the public by appointment.

Hours

Monday through Friday, 11:00–6:00.

Description of Women's Materials

There are some two hundred manuscripts of all playwrights who have had a reading or a production by the Women's Project.

Collection by Format

Audiotapes: yes
Manuscripts or archives: yes

Services

Telephone reference: yes

WORKING WOMEN'S INSTITUTE

see Cornell University/New York State School of Industrial and Labor Relations

168. YESHIVA UNIVERSITY

Hedi Steinberg Library
245 Lexington Avenue
New York, New York 10016

Telephone Number

(212) 340-7720

Contact Person

Edith Lubetski.

Objectives of Library or Information Center

To provide support for an undergraduate curriculum in general studies and Jewish studies.

Access Privileges

Open to Yeshiva University students and faculty; open to the public for reference use only. METRO referral card honored.

Hours

Monday through Wednesday, 9:00 A.M.–12:30 A.M.; Thursday, 9:00 A.M.–10:45 P.M.; Friday, 9:00–1:00; Sunday, 12:00–10:45.

Description of Women's Materials

Yeshiva University has a general collection of women's studies with special emphasis on women in literature. There is a special collection on Jewish women.

Collection by Format

Books and monographs: 500
Phonograph records: yes

There is a Judaica vertical file and a pamphlet file.

Services

Borrowing privileges: yes
Photocopying: yes
Telephone reference: yes

Interlibrary loan: yes
Reading room: yes
Audiovisual facilities: yes

169. YIVO INSTITUTE FOR JEWISH RESEARCH

1048 Fifth Avenue
New York, New York 10028

Telephone Number

(212) 535-6700, ext. 24

Contact Person

Dina Abramowicz, Librarian.

Objectives of Library or Information Center

To collect historical and current materials on Jewish subjects.

Access Privileges

Open to the public.

Hours

Monday, Tuesday, Thursday, Friday, 9:30–5:30.

Description of Women's Materials

The subject catalog on Jewish women includes the following topics: bibliography, biography (collective and individual), memoirs, autobiographies, historical sources, humorous treatment, women and Christianity, women and Judaism, Hasidism, literature, and women in various countries. Additionally, the classified catalog includes entries for the Holocaust, women in the Holocaust, labor, women in the labor movement, literature, and women in literature.

Collection by Format

Books and monographs: ca. 500   Reprints: yes
Pamphlets: yes   Archives: yes
Current serial titles: 3

Services

Telephone reference: yes   Photocopying: yes
Reading room: yes   Audiovisual facilities: yes

Publications

Finding aids/guides: Alphabetical and classified card catalogs.

YM—YWHA ARCHIVES (92ND STREET)

see 92nd Street YM—YWHA Archives

170. YWCA NATIONAL BOARD

Library and Archives
726 Broadway
New York, New York 10003

Telephone Number

(212) 614-2716

Contact Person

Elizabeth Norris, Librarian/YWCA Historian.

Objectives of Library or Information Center

Library: to provide current information on women, especially American women, to professional staff and members of the National Board.
Archives: to serve serious scholars pursuing subjects related to the YWCA and its role in effecting social change.

Access Privileges

Open to non-National Board users by appointment only.

Hours

Library: Monday through Friday, 9:00–4:00.
Archives: Monday and Tuesday, 9:00–4:00.

Description of Women's Materials

1) Library: contemporary books, pamphlets, periodicals on women, women's socialization and sex roles, physical and mental health, history, legal status, communications, feminist theory, specific cultural, ethnic, and racial groups, etc.
2) Archives: primary and secondary sources on the YWCA in the United States, 1860 to the present, including program, local community studies, stands on social and economic issues, etc. The publications of the Womans Press, 1918–1955, are also included.

Collection by Format

Books and monographs: ca. 6,000
Current serial titles: ca. 300
Pamphlets: ca. 3,000
Microfilm reels: 381
Slides: ca. 200
Oral history: 20 tapes

Manuscripts or archives: 395 linear feet
Government documents: ca. 20 series
Archival photographs: ca. 1400

The Archives include the history of the Public Affairs Department, 1920–80 (about 65 linear feet), concerning civil and democratic rights, discrimination, disarmament, labor, health and welfare issues, minorities, right-wing attacks, housing, poverty, social security, etc. It includes supporting documents of other nonprofit groups and government bodies.

Services

Photocopying: yes
Interlibrary loan: yes
Reading room: yes

Publications

Accession lists: yes
Bibliographies: *Forecasts of Trends Affecting Women,* an annual review based on selected year-end issues of periodicals, designed for the use of National YWCA consultants.
Finding aids/guides: *Inventory to the Records Files, Accession No. One; Topical Inventory to Photographs in YWCA Archives; Subject Index to YWCA Historical Publications.*

Additional Resources

In process: *Inventory of Artifacts, Memorabilia, and Posters*

Additional Publications

Historical Fact Sheets on the YWCA and Selected Women's Issues: The YWCA Advances Women's Rights, From Juniors to Women (teen movement), *On Their Own* (working women), *Diary of a Volunteer, Women and Children First* (day care), *Twenty Firsts* (landmark services originated by the YWCA). The Fact Sheets are one-page, back-to-back, intended for wide distribution to conferences and workshops and as background information for students preparing term papers, reports, or theses on the YWCA. They are preliminary indicators of archival holdings for more advanced researchers.

171. YWCA OF THE CITY OF NEW YORK

Archives Center
610 Lexington Avenue
New York, New York 10022

Telephone Number

(212) 735-9798

Contact Person

Lenore Parker.

Objectives of Library or Information Center

To develop a coherent archival program that will identify and preserve the historically significant records of the YWCA of the City of New York.

Access Privileges

Open to interested researchers by appointment.

Description of Women's Materials

The collection contains records created by the various units and departments of the YWCA. The records reflect activities connected with providing services to women for which the YWCA carried on an advocacy role: working women, interracial work, teen work, and public affairs.

Collection by Format

Books and monographs: yes
Reprints, clippings: yes
Pamphlets: yes

Oral history: yes
Manuscripts or archives: yes

SUBJECT INDEX

Numerals refer to entry numbers, not page numbers.

The Feminist Press at The City University of New York offers alternatives in education and in literature. Founded in 1970, this nonprofit, tax-exempt educational and publishing organization works to eliminate sexual stereotypes in books and schools and to provide literature with a broad vision of human potential. The publishing program includes reprints of important works by women, feminist biographies of women, and nonsexist children's books. Curricular materials, bibliographies, directories, and a quarterly journal provide information and support for students and teachers of women's studies. In-service projects help to transform teaching methods and curricula. Through publications and projects, The Feminist Press contributes to the rediscovery of the history of women and the emergence of a more humane society.

NEW AND FORTHCOMING BOOKS

Carrie Chapman Catt: A Public Life, by Jacqueline Van Voris. $24.95 cloth.
Competition: A Feminist Taboo? edited by Valerie Miner and Helen E. Longino. Foreword by Nell Irvin Painter. $29.95 cloth, $12.95 paper.
Daughter of Earth, a novel by Agnes Smedley. Foreword by Alice Walker. Afterword by Nancy Hoffman. $8.95 paper.
Doctor Zay, a novel by Elizabeth Stuart Phelps. Afterword by Michael Sartisky. $8.95 paper.
Get Smart: A Woman's Guide to Equality on Campus, by S. Montana Katz and Veronica Vieland. $29.95 cloth, $9.95 paper.
Harem Years: The Memoirs of an Egyptian Feminist, 1879–1924, by Huda Shaarawi. Translated and edited by Margot Badran. $29.95 cloth, $9.95 paper.
Leaving Home, a novel by Elizabeth Janeway. New Foreword by the author. Afterword by Rachel M. Brownstein. $8.95 paper.
Lone Voyagers: Academic Women in Coeducational Universities, 1869–1937, edited by Geraldine J. Clifford. $29.95 cloth, $12.95 paper.
My Mother Marries, a novel by Moa Martinson. Translated and introduced by Margaret S. Lacy. $8.95 paper.
Sultana's Dream and Selections from The Secluded Ones, by Rokeya Sakhawat Hossain. Edited and translated by Roushan Jahan. Afterword by Hanna Papanek. $16.95 cloth, $6.95 paper.
Turning the World Upside Down: The Anti-Slavery Convention of American Women Held in New York City, May 9–12, 1837. Introduction by Dorothy Sterling. $2.95 paper.
With Wings: An Anthology of Literature by and about Women with Disabilities, edited by Marsha Saxton and Florence Howe. $29.95 cloth, $12.95 paper.
Women Activists: Challenging the Abuse of Power, by Anne Witte Garland. Introduction by Frances T. Farenthold. Foreword by Ralph Nader. $29.95 cloth, $9.95 paper.
Writing Red: An Anthology of American Women Writers, 1930–1940, edited by Charlotte Nekola and Paula Rabinowitz. Foreword by Toni Morrison. $29.95 cloth, $12.95 paper.

FICTION CLASSICS

Between Mothers and Daughters: Stories across a Generation, edited by Susan Koppelman. $9.95 paper.
Brown Girl, Brownstones, a novel by Paule Marshall. Afterword by Mary Helen Washington. $8.95 paper.
Call Home the Heart, a novel of the thirties, by Fielding Burke. Introduction by Alice Kessler-Harris and Paul Lauter and afterwords by Sylvia J. Cook and Anna W. Shannon. $9.95 paper.
Cassandra, by Florence Nightingale. Introduction by Myra Stark. Epilogue by Cynthia MacDonald. $4.50 paper.
The Changelings, a novel by Jo Sinclair. Afterwords by Nellie McKay, and Johnnetta B. Cole and Elizabeth H. Oakes; biographical note by Elisabeth Sandberg. $8.95 paper.
The Convert, a novel by Elizabeth Robins. Introduction by Jane Marcus. $8.95 paper.
Daddy Was a Number Runner, a novel by Louise Meriwether. Foreword by James Baldwin and afterword by Nellie McKay. $8.95 paper.
Daughter of the Hills: A Woman's Part in the Coal Miners' Struggle, a novel of the thirties, by

Myra Page. Introduction by Alice Kessler-Harris and Paul Lauter and afterword by Deborah S. Rosenfelt. $8.95 paper.

An Estate of Memory, a novel by Ilona Karmel. Afterword by Ruth K. Angress. $11.95 paper.

Guardian Angel and Other Stories, by Margery Latimer. Afterwords by Nancy Loughridge, Meridel Le Sueur, and Louis Kampf. $8.95 paper.

I Love Myself when I Am Laughing . . . and Then Again when I Am Looking Mean and Impressive: A Zora Neale Hurston Reader, edited by Alice Walker. Introduction by Mary Helen Washington. $9.95 paper.

Life in the Iron Mills and Other Stories, by Rebecca Harding Davis. Biographical interpretation by Tillie Olsen. $7.95 paper.

The Living Is Easy, a novel by Dorothy West. Afterword by Adelaide M. Cromwell. $9.95 paper.

The Other Woman: Stories of Two Women and a Man, edited by Susan Koppelman. $9.95 paper.

The Parish and the Hill, a novel by Mary Doyle Curran. Afterword by Anne Halley. $8.95 paper.

Reena and Other Stories, selected short stories by Paule Marshall. $8.95 paper.

Ripening: Selected Work, 1927–1980, 2nd edition, by Meridel Le Sueur. Edited with an introduction by Elaine Hedges. $9.95 paper.

Rope of Gold, a novel of the thirties, by Josephine Herbst. Introduction by Alice Kessler-Harris and Paul Lauter and afterword by Elinor Langer. $9.95 paper.

The Silent Partner, a novel by Elizabeth Stuart Phelps. Afterword by Mari Jo Buhle and Florence Howe. $8.95 paper.

Swastika Night, a novel by Katharine Burdekin. Introduction by Daphne Patai. $8.95 paper.

This Child's Gonna Live, a novel by Sarah E. Wright. Appreciation by John Oliver Killens. $9.95 paper.

The Unpossessed, a novel of the thirties, by Tess Slesinger. Introduction by Alice Kessler-Harris and Paul Lauter and afterword by Janet Sharistanian. $9.95 paper.

Weeds, a novel by Edith Summers Kelley. Afterword by Charlotte Goodman. $8.95 paper.

The Wide, Wide World, a novel by Susan Warner. Afterword by Jane Tompkins. $29.95 cloth, $11.95 paper.

A Woman of Genius, a novel by Mary Austin. Afterword by Nancy Porter. $9.95 paper.

Women and Appletrees, a novel by Moa Martinson. Translated from the Swedish and with an afterword by Margaret S. Lacy. $8.95 paper.

Women Working: An Anthology of Stories and Poems, edited and with an introduction by Nancy Hoffman and Florence Howe. $9.95 paper.

The Yellow Wallpaper, by Charlotte Perkins Gilman. Afterword by Elaine Hedges. $4.50 paper.

OTHER TITLES

Antoinette Brown Blackwell: A Biography, by Elizabeth Cazden. $24.95 cloth, $12.95 paper.

All the Women Are White, All the Blacks Are Men, but Some of Us Are Brave: Black Women's Studies, edited by Gloria T. Hull, Patricia Bell Scott, and Barbara Smith. $12.95 paper.

Black Foremothers: Three Lives, by Dorothy Sterling. $9.95 paper.

Complaints and Disorders: The Sexual Politics of Sickness, by Barbara Ehrenreich and Deirdre English. $3.95 paper.

The Cross-Cultural Study of Women, edited by Margot I. Duley and Mary I. Edwards. $29.95 cloth, $12.95 paper.

A Day at a Time: The Diary Literature of American Women from 1764 to the Present, edited and with an introduction by Margo Culley. $29.95 cloth, $12.95 paper.

The Defiant Muse: French Feminist Poems from the Middle Ages to the Present, a bilingual anthology edited and with an introduction by Domna C. Stanton. $29.95 cloth, $11.95 paper.

The Defiant Muse: German Feminist Poems from the Middle Ages to the Present, a bilingual anthology edited and with an introduction by Susan L. Cocalis. $29.95 cloth, $11.95 paper.

The Defiant Muse: Hispanic Feminist Poems from the Middle Ages to the Present, a bilingual anthology edited and with an introduction by Angel Flores and Kate Flores. $29.95 cloth, $11.95 paper.

The Defiant Muse: Italian Feminist Poems from the Middle Ages to the Present, a bilingual anthology edited by Beverly Allen, Muriel Kittel, and Keala Jane Jewell, and with an introduction by Beverly Allen. $29.95 cloth, $11.95 paper.

Feminist Resources for Schools and Colleges: A Guide to Curricular Materials, 3rd edition, compiled and edited by Anne Chapman. $12.95 paper.

Household and Kin, by Amy Swerdlow, Renate Bridenthal, Joan Kelly, and Phyllis Vine. $9.95 paper.

How to Get Money for Research, by Mary Rubin and the Business and Professional Women's Foundation. Foreword by Mariam Chamberlain. $6.95 paper.

In Her Own Image: Women Working in the Arts, edited and with an introduction by Elaine Hedges and Ingrid Wendt. $9.95 paper.

Integrating Women's Studies into the Curriculum: A Guide and Bibliography, by Betty Schmitz. $9.95 paper.

Käthe Kollwitz: Woman and Artist, by Martha Kearns, $9.95 paper.

Las Mujeres: Conversations from a Hispanic Community, by Nan Elsasser, Kyle MacKenzie, and Yvonne Tixier y Vigil. $9.95 paper.

Lesbian Studies: Present and Future, edited by Margaret Cruikshank. $9.95 paper.

Mother to Daughter, Daughter to Mother: A Daybook and Reader, selected and shaped by Tillie Olsen. $9.95 paper.

Moving the Mountain: Women Working for Social Change, by Ellen Cantarow with Susan Gushee O'Malley and Sharon Hartman Strom. $9.95 paper.

Out of the Bleachers: Writings on Women and Sport, edited and with an introduction by Stephanie L. Twin. $10.95 paper.

Portraits of Chinese Women in Revolution, by Agnes Smedley. Edited and with an introduction by Jan MacKinnon and Steve MacKinnon and an afterword by Florence Howe. $10.95 paper.

Reconstructing American Literature: Courses, Syllabi, Issues, edited by Paul Lauter. $10.95 paper.

Rights and Wrongs: Women's Struggle for Legal Equality, 2nd edition, by Susan Cary Nichols, Alice M. Price, and Rachel Rubin. $7.95 paper.

Salt of the Earth, screenplay by Michael Wilson with historical commentary by Deborah Silverton Rosenfelt. $10.95 paper.

These Modern Women: Autobiographical Essays from the Twenties, edited with an introduction by Elaine Showalter. $8.95 paper.

Witches, Midwives, and Nurses: A History of Women Healers, by Barbara Ehrenreich and Deirdre English. $3.95 paper.

With These Hands: Women Working on the Land, edited with an introduction by Joan M. Jensen. $9.95 paper.

The Woman and the Myth: Margaret Fuller's Life and Writings, by Bell Gale Chevigny. $8.95 paper.

Woman's "True" Profession: Voices from the History of Teaching, edited with an introduction by Nancy Hoffman. $9.95 paper.

Women Have Always Worked: A Historical Overview, by Alice Kessler-Harris. $9.95 paper.

For a free catalog, write to The Feminist Press at The City University of New York, 311 East 94 Street, New York, NY 10128. Send individual book orders to The Talman Company, Inc., 150 Fifth Avenue, New York, NY 10011. Please include $1.75 for postage and handling for one book, $.75 for each additional.